CAMPAIGN 399

PHILIPPINES NAVAL CAMPAIGN 1944–45

The Battles After Leyte Gulf

MARK STILLE

ILLUSTRATED BY ADAM TOOBY
Series editor Nikolai Bogdanovic

OSPREY PUBLISHING
Bloomsbury Publishing Plc
Kemp House, Chawley Park, Cumnor Hill, Oxford OX2 9PH, UK
29 Earlsfort Terrace, Dublin 2, Ireland
1385 Broadway, 5th Floor, New York, NY 10018, USA
E-mail: info@ospreypublishing.com
www.ospreypublishing.com

OSPREY is a trademark of Osprey Publishing Ltd

First published in Great Britain in 2024

A catalog record for this book is available from the British Library.

ISBN: PB 9781472856999; eBook 9781472856982; ePDF 9781472856968;
XML 9781472856975

24 25 26 27 28   10 9 8 7 6 5 4 3 2 1

Maps by Bounford.com
3D BEVs by Paul Kime
Index by Zoe Ross
Typeset by PDQ Digital Media Solutions, Bungay, UK
Printed and bound in India by Replika Press Private Ltd.

Osprey Publishing supports the Woodland Trust, the UK's leading woodland
conservation charity.

FSC
www.fsc.org
MIX
Paper from
responsible sources
FSC® C016779

To find out more about our authors and books visit
www.ospreypublishing.com. Here you will find extracts, author
interviews, details of forthcoming events and the option to sign up for
our newsletter.

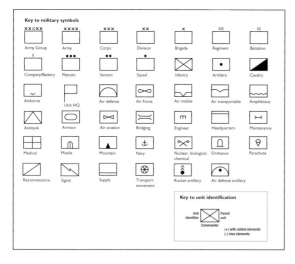

Artist's note

Readers can find out more about the work of battlescene illustrator Adam
Tooby by visiting the following website:

www.adamtooby.com

Photographs

Unless otherwise indicated, the photographs that appear in this work are
Public Domain.

Acronyms

AAF	(US) Army Air Forces
ASW	antisubmarine warfare
CAP	combat air patrol
IJA	Imperial Japanese Army
IJAAF	Imperial Japanese Army Air Force
IJN	Imperial Japanese Navy
LCI	Landing Craft, Infantry
LSD	Landing Ship, Dock
LSM	Landing Ship, Medium
LST	Landing Ship, Tank
nm	nautical mile
RAN	Royal Australian Navy
TF	Task Force
TG	Task Group
USN	United States Navy

Front cover main illustration: TF 38 ravages Japanese convoy
TA Number 3's cargo ships on November 11, 1944 as they approach
Leyte. (Adam Tooby)
Title page photograph: *LSM-20*, which sank on December 5, 1944
with the loss of eight crewmen and the wounding of nine more
during the US operation to land reinforcements 25 miles south of
Ormoc. (Naval Historical and Heritage Command)

CONTENTS

The American Conquest of the Philippines, 1944–45

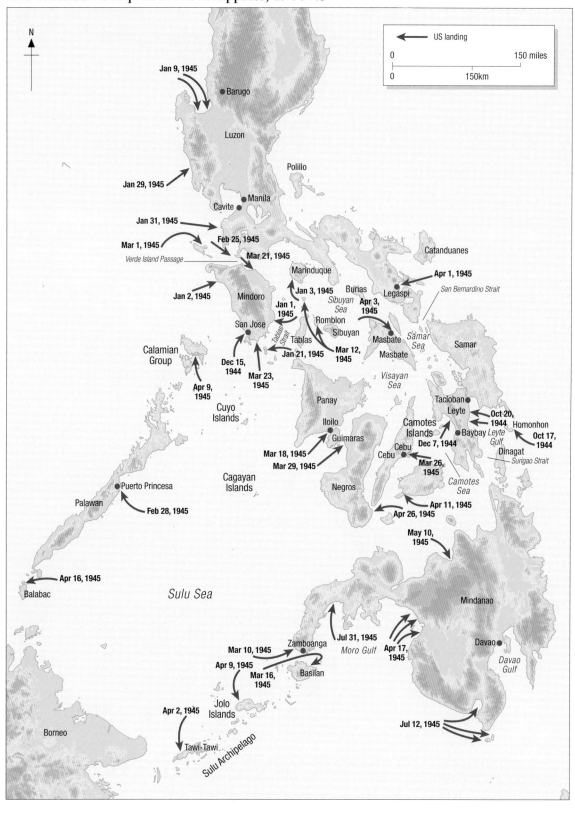

N

US landing

0   150 miles

0   150km

Jan 9, 1945

Barugo

Luzon

Polillo

Jan 29, 1945

Manila

Cavite

Jan 31, 1945

Feb 25, 1945

Mar 1, 1945

Verde Island Passage

Mar 21, 1945

Marinduque

Jan 3, 1945

Burias

Catanduanes

Apr 1, 1945

Legaspi

San Bernardino Strait

Jan 2, 1945

Mindoro

Jan 1, 1945

Sibuyan Sea

Apr 3, 1945

San Jose

Romblon

Tablas

Sibuyan

Masbate

Samar Sea

Samar

Mar 12, 1945

Masbate

Calamian Group

Dec 15, 1944

Mar 23, 1945

Tablas Strait

Jan 21, 1945

Visayan Sea

Apr 9, 1945

Cuyo Islands

Panay

Tacloban

Leyte

Oct 20, 1944

Homonhon

Iloilo

Camotes Islands

Baybay

Leyte Gulf

Oct 17, 1944

Guimaras

Cebu

Dec 7, 1944

Dinagat

Mar 18, 1945

Cebu

Surigao Strait

Mar 29, 1945

Mar 26, 1945

Camotes Sea

Cagayan Islands

Negros

Apr 11, 1945

Puerto Princesa

Apr 26, 1945

Palawan

May 10, 1945

Feb 28, 1945

Apr 16, 1945

Balabac

Sulu Sea

Mindanao

Davao

Zamboanga

Jul 31, 1945

Moro Gulf

Apr 17, 1945

Mar 10, 1945

Apr 9, 1945

Mar 16, 1945

Basilan

Davao Gulf

Jolo Islands

Apr 2, 1945

Borneo

Tawi-Tawi

Sulu Archipelago

Jul 12, 1945

ORIGINS OF THE CAMPAIGN

The naval operations and battles in the Philippines after the Battle of Leyte Gulf have become an afterthought in the history of the Pacific War. These battles have been overshadowed by the largest naval battle of the war fought on October 23–25, 1944 between the Imperial Japanese Navy (IJN) and the United States Navy (USN) as a result of the American invasion of Leyte in the central Philippines. The result was a smashing American victory in which the IJN was shattered as an effective fighting force. The battle left the IJN's surface fleet in disarray, crippled by heavy losses, with the remaining units suffering from lack of fuel. From this point forward, the IJN's land-based air forces carried the brunt of the struggle against the USN. However, the USN's signal victory at Leyte Gulf did not end the naval campaign for the Philippines. For the remainder of 1944, both sides maneuvered to reinforce their forces on Leyte, which the Imperial Japanese Army (IJA) had selected as the location for the decisive battle for the defense of the Philippines. Despite the fact that the USN had won a decisive victory against the IJN, it failed to follow up this success by securing the waters around Leyte. As a result, the IJN was able to move a large number of IJA units to Leyte despite an increasingly heavy toll inflicted on Japanese shipping due to American air attacks. In total, the IJN ran nine convoys to Leyte. After some initial success, these operations became too costly and the IJA troops on the island were left stranded.

The naval battle for Leyte was heavily influenced by the battle for the air space over and around the island. By November 1, the Japanese had regained air control of this region. Poor ground conditions prevented the Americans from completing airfields on Leyte and the USN's Fast Carrier Force—designated as Task Force (TF) 38 during this period—was unable to provide continuous coverage over the central Philippines due to the exhaustion of its aviators after being in action for several months without significant respite. Nevertheless, the weight of American air power made the Japanese position on Leyte perilous. The scale of Japanese shipping losses forced the suspension of Japanese convoys to Leyte in December. This was followed by an American landing on the western side of the island near the primary port being used by the Japanese for resupply operations. As the Americans slowly advanced across Leyte, they began to insert naval forces into Ormoc Bay on the west side of the island. This prompted two small naval clashes on December 3 and 12, 1944.

When the Americans landed on Leyte in October, the future course of operations in the Philippines was unclear. The USN and General Douglas MacArthur had different visions of the extent of follow-up operations in the

Philippines. MacArthur's vision prevailed, setting the Americans on a path of liberating the entire archipelago. This entailed a series of landings by the Seventh Fleet and the continued presence of TF 38 to provide cover. Though the IJN's surface force had been rendered ineffective at the Battle of Leyte Gulf, Japanese land-based aircraft remained a constant threat. This threat was intensified by the adoption of mass suicide attacks. Beginning during the Battle of Leyte Gulf with the opening salvos from a small group of suicide aircraft, the IJN's special attack (better known as kamikaze) effort expanded rapidly. It was joined by suicide attacks conducted by IJA air units.

Before the fighting was over on Leyte, the Americans were preparing a massive amphibious attack on Luzon, the ultimate prize for control of the Philippines. An intermediary objective was Mindoro Island, located in the western part of the central Philippines. The Americans landed on the island on December 15 against heavy air attacks with a significant participation of suicide units. The invasion of Mindoro prompted the largest IJN operation of the campaign when a force led by a heavy cruiser attempted to attack the beachhead and the shipping offshore. Though the attack took the Americans by surprise, it inflicted little damage and imposed no delay on the pace of the American advance.

Just as the Japanese had done in 1941 when they attacked the Philippines, the American return to Luzon focused on an amphibious landing in Lingayen Gulf in the western part of Luzon. The invasion force was subjected to eight days of intense kamikaze attacks, constituting the heaviest such attacks thus far in the war. Many ships were hit and damaged, and a much smaller number were sunk, but the landing on January 9, 1945 proceeded as planned. Unable to sustain their air forces in the region, the Japanese literally ran out of suicide aircraft and pilots. However, the invasion of Luzon provided a portent of things to come as the Americans contemplated future landings closer to Japan. Following the successful landing at Lingayen Gulf, the naval campaign for the Philippines continued on a smaller scale with a series of American landings throughout the archipelago.

CHRONOLOGY

1944

October 20   Americans land on Leyte.

October 23–26   Battle of Leyte Gulf; the IJN is crippled as an effective fighting force.

October 26   Japanese *TA Number 1* operation delivers 2,500 men to Leyte.

October 29–30   TF 38 suffers first kamikaze attack; three carriers are damaged.

November 1   Seventh Fleet suffers intense kamikaze attack inside Leyte Gulf; one destroyer sunk and three damaged.

November 2   *TA Number 2* lands 10,000 troops at Ormoc.

November 5   TF 38 launches major strikes on Luzon; heavy cruiser *Nachi* is sunk in Manila Bay.

November 9–10   *TA Number 4* lands almost 10,000 troops at Ormoc but suffers heavy losses.

November 11   TF 38 annihilates *TA Number 3*.

November 13   TF 38 attacks shipping in Manila Bay; one light cruiser and four destroyers are sunk.

November 24–25   *TA Number 5* fails to deliver any troops or supplies to Leyte.

November 27   Task Group (TG) 77.2 attacked by kamikazes inside Leyte Gulf; one battleship and two light cruisers are damaged.

November 28–30   All of *TA Number 6* is destroyed, but a small amount of supplies reach Leyte.

November 29   One battleship and two destroyers are struck by kamikazes in Leyte Gulf.

November 30–December 2   The three echelons of *TA Number 7* get limited amounts of troops and supplies to Leyte.

December 2   Battle of Ormoc Bay; the IJN and USN both lose a destroyer.

December 7   Americans land an amphibious force near Ormoc. The kamikaze response is fierce; one destroyer and a destroyer-transport are sunk, and another destroyer and a destroyer-transport are damaged.

TA Number 8 is shattered by air attack, but the Japanese get some 4,000 men ashore on Leyte with no heavy equipment or supplies.

December 10   Ormoc is captured. More shipping in Leyte Gulf is attacked by kamikazes.

December 11   USN reinforcement convoy for Ormoc is heavily attacked by kamikazes; one destroyer is sunk.

December 11–12   *TA Number 9*, the final convoy to Leyte, gets a small amount of troops and supplies to Leyte but suffers heavy losses.

December 13   Mindoro invasion force struck by kamikazes.

December 14–16   TF 38 attacks airfields on Luzon to suppress kamikazes threatening Mindoro invasion force.

December 15   Americans land on Mindoro; kamikazes sink two LSTs.

December 18   TF 38 encounters a typhoon and suffers heavy damage, including three destroyers sunk.

December 21   Mindoro reinforcement convoy attacked by kamikazes; two LSTs are sunk.

December 26–27	IJN San Jose Intrusion Force attacks Mindoro beachhead; Japanese lose one destroyer and inflict little damage.
December 28–January 4, 1945	Japanese air attacks continue on Mindoro reinforcement convoys; seven ships are sunk and another five damaged.

1945

January 3–4	TF 38 strikes targets on Formosa.
January 4	First kamikaze attacks on Luzon invasion force; escort carrier *Ommaney Bay* is sunk.
January 5	Kamikaze attacks on Luzon invasion force hit five ships, but only a small landing craft sinks.
January 6	Most intensive kamikaze attacks on the Luzon invasion force; 12 ships are hit, but only two destroyer-minesweepers are sunk or are deemed unrepairable.
January 6–7	TF 38 strikes targets on Luzon.
January 7	Two destroyer-minesweepers sunk by conventional air attack.
January 8–13	Continuing kamikaze attacks on the Luzon invasion force damage 22 more ships, including three escort carriers.
January 9	TF 38 strikes targets on Formosa and in the Ryukyus.
	Americans land at Lingayen Gulf.
January 12	TF 38 annihilates Japanese shipping in the South China Sea.
January 14	TF 38 strikes targets on Formosa.
January 16	TF 38 attacks focus on shipping at Hong Kong.
January 20	TF 38 departs the South China Sea.

January 21	TF 38 strikes targets on Formosa, and in the Pescadores and Ryukyus. Retaliation by kamikazes damages a fleet and a light carrier.
January 22	TF 38 strikes targets in the Ryukyus before heading to Ulithi.

OPPOSING COMMANDERS

UNITED STATES NAVY

Though obviously not a naval commander, the Philippines campaign was conducted under the direction of **General Douglas MacArthur** in his capacity as Supreme Commander, Southwest Pacific Area. The Seventh Fleet, commanded by Vice Admiral Thomas C. Kinkaid, was part of MacArthur's command. MacArthur worked well with Kinkaid and had real respect for Admiral William F. Halsey, commander of the Third Fleet, which was not part of MacArthur's command. For the most part, MacArthur let the Navy run the naval campaign. However, reflecting the general command friction between the Army and the Navy, MacArthur ordered that all communications between the Seventh Fleet and the Third Fleet go through his headquarters instead of directly to each other.

Admiral Ernest J. King exercised overall direction of USN strategy and worldwide resource allocation in his dual capacities as Commander-in-Chief, US Fleet and Chief of Naval Operations. He generally left direction of the Pacific campaign to **Admiral Chester W. Nimitz**, Commander-in-Chief, Pacific Fleet and Pacific Ocean Areas. During the Philippines campaign, Nimitz retained strategic control of the Third Fleet. He was known for letting his subordinates get on with the tasks they had been given, but exercised oversight of Halsey and at times curbed his overly aggressive planning.

Admiral William F. Halsey was in command of the powerful Third Fleet for most of Philippines campaign. He had just led his command to a great victory at the Battle of Leyte Gulf. His performance during the battle was generally poor, but he retained the support of King and Nimitz. During the Philippines campaign his carrier force was asked by MacArthur to remain on station for a month longer than planned.

The driving force behind the invasion of the Philippines was General Douglas MacArthur, Supreme Commander, Allied Forces, Southwest Pacific Area. He was ably assisted by his naval subordinates, among them Rear Admiral Daniel E. Barbey, Commander Amphibious Force, Seventh Fleet. In this photograph from September 15, 1944, MacArthur (center) and Barbey (left) inspect the invasion beaches at Morotai Island, Netherlands East Indies. (Naval Historical and Heritage Command)

Two of the USN's principal naval commanders during the Philippines campaign are shown in this photograph from December 24, 1944 aboard the battleship *New Jersey*. In the center is Admiral Chester Nimitz being greeted by Admiral William F. Halsey. As Commander-in-Chief Pacific Fleet, Nimitz had control of Halsey's Third Fleet. Several times during the campaign, Nimitz had to exert supervision over Halsey. (Naval Historical and Heritage Command)

Halsey doggedly supported MacArthur despite the exhaustion of this carrier force, to the point of exposing the Third Fleet to a damaging typhoon in December. Halsey and his staff were sloppy planners, and Halsey's command style did not readily accommodate advice from his subordinates. He was a supremely aggressive combat leader, an attribute again on display during the Philippines campaign.

Very early in the campaign, **Vice Admiral John S. McCain** assumed command of TF 38, the Third Fleet's fast carrier force. McCain replaced the well-respected and battle-tested Vice Admiral Marc Mitscher. McCain

The principal entity of Halsey's Third Fleet was TF 38, commanded by Vice Admiral John S. McCain, Sr. Here, Halsey decorates McCain with the Navy Cross aboard McCain's flagship *Hancock* on November 30, 1944. Working relations between the two were often tense. (Naval Historical and Heritage Command)

was not well received by his task force commanders or by Halsey. In contrast to the way Mitscher had smoothly run TF 38, McCain quickly became known for issuing vague or even contradictory orders. This ineptness irritated Halsey to the point that in January 1945 he set up a command structure for TF 38 that bypassed McCain entirely. His task force commanders resented his new concepts, which they thought failed to take their recent experiences into account. On balance, McCain was merely an observer given Halsey's desire to be both a fleet and task force commander. TF 38 comprised a variable number of subordinate task groups with each commanded by experienced and capable officers. TG 38.1 was under the command of **Rear Admiral A.E. Montgomery**, who relieved McCain when he assumed command of TF 38 on October 30. On December 25, Montgomery was hurt in a boating incident at Ulithi and was relieved by **Rear Admiral Arthur Radford**. He was highly regarded and in 1953 became the Chairman of the Joint Chiefs of Staff. TG 38.2 was led by **Rear Admiral Gerald F. Bogan** and TG 38.3 by **Rear Admiral Frederick C. Sherman**. Sherman was the senior task force commander and resented the arrival of McCain, which he and others thought was the result of King's interference.

Commander of the Seventh Fleet was **Vice Admiral Thomas C. Kinkaid**. His career was resurrected in 1943 when he was given a backwater command in the North Pacific, but promptly demonstrated an ability to work with the US Army. This led to his assignment as Commander, Allied Naval Forces Southwest Pacific Area and Commander of the Seventh Fleet under MacArthur. The Seventh Fleet became known as "MacArthur's Navy" following a string of successful amphibious operations on New Guinea. Kinkaid was present at the Battle of Leyte Gulf, where he and his staff did not

Pictured as a captain in 1938, Rear Admiral Frederick Sherman was an experienced carrier commander and in command of TG 38.3 during the campaign. As senior task group commander, he took over TF 38 in November during McCain's absence. During this time, he led the devastating strikes against a Japanese reinforcement convoy headed for Leyte and shipping in Manila, which severely limited the IJN's ability to reinforce and resupply Leyte. (Naval Historical and Heritage Command)

Vice Admiral Thomas C. Kinkaid was the commander of the Seventh Fleet throughout the campaign. He had the benefit of very capable subordinates. For the invasion of the Philippines, amphibious forces were pulled from the Third and Seventh fleets. In this view, Kinkaid (center) confers with Vice Admiral Theodore S. Wilkinson (left), Commander Amphibious Force, Third Fleet, and Rear Admiral Daniel E. Barbey (right), Commander Amphibious Force, Seventh Fleet, before the invasion of Leyte. This same team planned and executed the Luzon invasion. (Naval Historical and Heritage Command)

prove adept at major fleet operations. Throughout the rest of the Philippines campaign he resisted returning ships to the Pacific Fleet from where they had been borrowed for the Leyte and Luzon operations. Perhaps because of his experience at Leyte when he allowed part of his fleet to be surprised by a force of heavy Japanese warships, he was overly concerned with the possibility of another appearance of major IJN units. This led to an overconcentration of major warships in the Philippines, which was unnecessary.

Kinkaid's principal subordinate was **Rear Admiral Jesse B. Oldendorf**. He had played a prominent role at the Battle of Surigao Strait and proved just as capable during the rest of the Philippines campaign. Kinkaid's amphibious force commanders played an important role in the campaign. **Vice Admiral Theodore S. Wilkinson** and **Rear Admiral Daniel E. Barbey** were the principal planners of the Mindoro and Luzon invasions. Wilkinson was from the Pacific Fleet while Barbey had made his mark in the Seventh Fleet. Kinkaid wanted Barbey to command the amphibious forces in the Philippines campaign, but Nimitz preferred Wilkinson, who was more senior and more experienced. Under a compromise arrangement, both commanders took part in the invasion of Luzon under Kinkaid's command. Barbey was the master of small-scale amphibious operations, conducting a total of 56 assaults by the end of the war. **Rear Admiral Arthur D. Struble** was one of Barbey's amphibious commanders. He was given the task of running resupply convoys to Ormoc and then was given command of the Mindoro invasion.

IMPERIAL JAPANESE NAVY

At the Battle of Leyte Gulf, the IJN's surface forces were eviscerated. The battle had been fought under the direction of the commander of the Combined Fleet, **Admiral Toyoda Soemu**. In spite of this drubbing, he retained his post throughout the Philippines campaign, though he had little impact on how it was fought. Some of the other principal commanders from the Battle of Leyte Gulf had tangential roles in the Philippines campaign. **Vice Admiral**

FAR LEFT
The principal surface force in the Southwest Area Fleet was the Second Diversionary Attack Force under Vice Admiral Shima Kiyohide. After Shima's flagship was sunk in Manila Bay on November 5, Shima left the Philippines. When what was left of his force was committed against the Mindoro beachhead in December, Shima delegated command to a subordinate. (Naval Historical and Heritage Command)

LEFT
Rear Admiral Kimura Masatomi had seen much action earlier in the war. As a destroyer squadron commander he led the ill-fated convoy in the Battle of the Bismarck Sea, in which he was wounded on March 2, 1943. A few months later, he executed the brilliant evacuation from Kiska Island in the Aleutians. As commander of the Second Destroyer Squadron, he took part in the *TA* operation and then led the San Jose Intrusion Force. (Naval Historical and Heritage Command)

Kurita Takeo had been commander of the First Diversion Attack Force with almost all of the IJN's heavy surface ships. He declined to execute Toyoda's plan for the immolation of his entire fleet, so saved part of it. The remnants of his fleet played no part in the Philippines campaign.

Japanese naval forces in the Philippines were under the command of the Southwest Area Fleet led by **Vice Admiral Mikawa Guinichi**. He was the victor of the Battle of Savo Island and longtime nemesis of Allied forces in the Solomons. His deteriorating health forced him to relinquish command of Southwest Area Fleet to **Vice Admiral Okochi Denshichi** around November 1. Okochi had commanded the China Area Fleet earlier in the war and came to Manila from the post of Superintendent of the Naval War College. Upon arrival, he had to immediately support the ill-conceived notion of fighting the decisive ground battle in the Philippines on Leyte instead of Luzon. Despite his slender resources, he was successful in moving considerable ground forces to Leyte at the expense of most of his fleet. Though he set up the defense of Manila with IJN ground forces which resulted in the slaughter of an estimated 100,000 Filipino civilians, he was not charged with war crimes. He surrendered on September 3, 1945. One of Okochi's most senior subordinates was **Vice Admiral Shima Kiyohide**, who led the Second Diversion Attack Force during the Battle of Leyte Gulf. His force survived largely intact, but Shima did not play any further role in the Philippines campaign.

Rear Admiral Kimura Masatomi was an experienced destroyer commander who had taken part in the Battle of Leyte Gulf under Shima's command. He was given command of one of the most important reinforcement convoys to Leyte. In March 1943, he had commanded a similar operation at the Battle of the Bismarck Sea, in which his convoy had been annihilated. In December, Kimura was given command of the San Jose Intrusion Force in the largest offensive IJN operation of the campaign. **Rear Admiral Matsuyama Mitsuharu** commanded the 7th Convoy Escort Group which escorted the convoy carrying the IJA's 1st Division from Shanghai all the way to Ormoc. He was experienced at escorting troop movements and had enjoyed success in such operations during the New Guinea campaign.

Vice Admiral Fukudome Shigeru was one of the more interesting IJN command figures. In April 1944, he was captured by Filipino guerillas after his aircraft crashed in a storm. He was released and returned to duty in spite of his period of captivity. Appointed to command the Second Air Fleet on Formosa in June, he and his formation moved to Luzon during the Battle of Leyte Gulf and remained there throughout the Philippines campaign until his command was virtually annihilated. He initially refused to let his pilots take part in kamikaze tactics but was quickly convinced of their necessity. (Naval Historical and Heritage Command)

The most important component of the Combined Fleet during the Philippines campaign was its land-based air forces. Commander of the First Air Fleet was **Vice Admiral Onishi Takijiro,** who organized the first kamikaze unit before the Battle of Leyte Gulf. He remained a fierce advocate for "special attack" tactics until the end of the war and committed ritual suicide before Japan's formal surrender. **Vice Admiral Fukudome Shigeru** was commander of the Formosa-based Second Air Fleet before the Battle of Leyte Gulf. He was not an advocate of kamikaze attacks until it was obvious that conventional tactics were utterly hopeless. He ended the war in Singapore as an area fleet commander.

Vice Admiral Onishi Takijiro provided the impetus for the first organized kamikaze attacks on October 25, 1944. His career was filled with milestones such as being one of the IJN's first aviators, being considered one of the IJN's foremost authorities on air power, being assigned as one of the first officers to study the proposed attack on Pearl Harbor, and, finally, advocating against Japan's surrender and proposing that Japan's entire male population be forced into the Special Attack Corps. After the end of the Philippines campaign, he continued the kamikaze fight from Formosa. In this view he gives one of the earliest special attack pilots a ceremonial cup of sake. (Naval Historical and Heritage Command)

OPPOSING FORCES

UNITED STATES NAVY

The Third Fleet

The USN's premier striking force, and in fact the most powerful striking force in the world in October 1944, was the Third Fleet. The centerpiece of this huge force was TF 38. At the start of the campaign, TF 38 was in its standard four-task-group organization. This changed in December due to several carriers being damaged by kamikaze attack and the desire to create larger task forces with more escorts to combat the threat. Each task group was a powerful striking force in itself with between one and three Essex-class fleet carriers and usually two Independence-class light carriers.

Each task group had a support force with two or three fast battleships, several cruisers (either light, heavy, or antiaircraft) and a large number of destroyers. The screen provided antiaircraft protection for the carriers. By late 1944, USN antiaircraft capabilities were well developed and took a high toll on attacking Japanese aircraft. Against kamikazes it was a different story, since the most numerous 20mm and 40mm guns lacked the stopping power to prevent kamikazes from hitting the ship after they had begun their final dive.

The backbone of the Fast Carrier Force was its Essex-class carriers. They possessed unparalleled striking power and were robust enough to take damage and stay in action. In this view, *Essex* is about to be hit by a "Judy" kamikaze on November 25, 1944. The flaming Judy struck near the carrier's forward elevator. In the background is a Cleveland-class light cruiser. Six Essex-class ships were hit by kamikazes during the campaign but none were placed in any danger of sinking. (Naval Historical and Heritage Command)

A Grumman F6F Hellcat taking off from *Lexington* in mid-October during the raid on Formosa. The Hellcat was dominant during the Philippines campaign by virtue of its speed, firepower, and toughness, combined with the generally excellent training level of its pilots. (Naval Historical and Heritage Command)

The backbone of TF 38 was its Essex-class carriers. These 37,000-ton ships were the most powerful of the war. They were large enough to carry up to 100 aircraft and mount a large defensive antiaircraft battery, and possessed good speed and endurance. The Independence-class light carriers were converted from light cruisers. With their air group of 33 aircraft, they were useful complements to the fleet carriers.

At the same time the number of task groups was being adjusted, the organization of fleet carrier air groups was also changing. The intensity of kamikaze attacks made it clear that more fighters were needed for air defense and air-superiority missions. At the beginning of the campaign each Essex-class carrier carried a fighter squadron with 38 F6F-3 Hellcats, a dive-bomber squadron with 36 SB2C Helldiver dive-bombers, and a torpedo squadron with 18 TBF/TBM-1 Avengers. By December 1944, fleet carrier groups underwent a transformation to increase the number of fighters. The new organization called for a much larger fighter squadron of 73 aircraft, a much smaller dive-bomber squadron of 15 aircraft, and a torpedo squadron with 15 aircraft.

The huge fighter squadron was manned by 110 pilots. It proved to be too burdensome for administrative purposes and was soon split into two. One of these was a purely fighter squadron and the other a fighter-bomber squadron in which many of the pilots were former Helldiver pilots. In January 1945, another effort was made to get more fighters on the flight decks. Two squadrons

A Curtiss SB2C-3 Helldiver from *Hancock* photographed along the coast of Formosa on October 13, 1944. After a painful gestation period, the Helldiver became a powerful attack aircraft by late 1944. Its days as a mainstay in carrier air groups were limited by the need to get more fighters on carrier decks to counter the kamikaze threat. (Naval Historical and Heritage Command)

of Marine Corps F4U Corsairs, totaling 91 aircraft, were embarked on *Essex* and *Wasp*. All the Helldivers were removed and only 15 Avengers remained.

Efforts to move more fighters on carrier decks meant there were more fighters for combat air patrol (CAP) duties and to escort strikes. The reduction in the number of dive-bombers did not result in a degradation of offensive capabilities; in fact, the number of strike aircraft increased. The F6F-5 version of the Hellcat could carry 1,000 pounds of bombs and six 5-inch rockets in addition to its already heavy armament of six .50-caliber machine guns. In addition to being a very capable fighter-bomber, the Hellcat was a superlative fighter. It possessed superior protection, speed, and firepower to its Japanese counterpart, the A6M "Zero" fighter. Most importantly, its pilots were much better trained.

Fatigue was a real problem for TF 38 by the end of October. Two of the task groups had departed Ulithi on October 6 and had been in constant action since. TG 38.4 had been at sea for 64 days by October 30 with only a 3½-day break at Ulithi. Over 50 percent of *Franklin*'s crew were suffering from heat rash. On *Wasp*, Air Group 14 had only 30 of 131 pilots fit for further duty according to the assessment of the flight surgeon. Halsey was forced to deal with the constant problem of meeting mission requirements while finding time for his task groups to get brief periods of rest. He invariably came down on the side of mission requirements.

An unsung, but critical, part of the Third Fleet was TG 30.8, the At Sea Logistics Group. Assigned an imposing number of supply ships, it provided TF 38 the capability to remain at sea for an extended period. For example, in December 1944 TG 30.8 possessed 29 fleet oilers, seven ammunition ships, seven fleet tugs, and eight escort carriers carrying replacement aircraft and pilots for the fleet carriers. Escort was provided by 14 destroyers and 25 destroyer escorts. It was typical for TF 38 to refuel every three days.

The Seventh Fleet

Before the invasion of the Philippines, Kinkaid's command was a backwater fleet. Nimitz ensured that major units were not assigned to the Seventh Fleet for fear they would fall under MacArthur's control. Nevertheless, the Seventh Fleet continued to grow, and by April 1944 it included 215 ships and craft for the invasion of Hollandia. For this major operation, Nimitz provided cover in the form of TF 38. For the Leyte invasion, many Pacific Fleet units, including six old battleships, several cruisers, and 18 escort carriers, augmented the Seventh Fleet.

On October 29, in the aftermath of the Battle of Leyte Gulf, Kinkaid reorganized his surface combatant force. Since it had been in constant alert or action since mid-October, as many ships as possible were sent to Ulithi for maintenance and rest. Enough ships remained in Leyte Gulf to deal with any potential sortie by the IJN's surviving surface ships. These included battleships *California*, *Mississippi*, and *Pennsylvania*; the Australian heavy cruiser *Shropshire*; light cruisers *Boise*, *Nashville*, and *Phoenix*; and 13 destroyers. For the Mindoro invasion, Kinkaid assembled a large force of 180 ships and craft. The Heavy Covering and Carrier Group was stationed in the Sulu Sea for support. This was composed of six escort carriers, three battleships, three light cruisers, and 18 destroyers.

Admiral Struble, in overall command of the operation, exercised direct command of the landing force known as the Mindoro Attack Force.

Amphibious shipping included 30 Landing Ship, Tank craft (LST—an almost 4,000-ton full-load ship capable of discharging cargo and vehicles directly on the beach), 12 Landing Ship, Medium (LSM—a 914-ton ship also capable of beach landings), 31 Landing Craft, Infantry (LCI—a 400-ton full-load craft capable of embarking 180–210 troops), 17 minesweepers, and 14 smaller craft. These embarked an invasion force of over 16,500 men and 27,600 tons of supplies and equipment. Direct escort was comprised of Struble's flagship, the light cruiser *Nashville*, and 12 destroyers.

For the Lingayen operation the amphibious attack force included 420 ships and craft. Oldendorf's Bombardment and Fire Support Group included almost as many ships with six old battleships and nine cruisers. An important part of the operation was the Escort Carrier Group. For the invasion of Luzon, this force had grown to 18 escort carriers, with a nominal air group of 24 FM-1 Wildcat fighters and nine Avengers. The inclusion of the vulnerable escort carriers in the face of a growing kamikaze threat was necessary because of the failure of the Army Air Force (AAF) to move significant strength to the airfields on Leyte as planned.

IMPERIAL JAPANESE NAVY

The IJN suffered crippling losses in the Battle of Leyte Gulf. Many of those ships that weren't sunk were damaged. At the end of the battle fuel and munitions were in short supply. Admiral Toyoda had little left to work with to mount a naval defense of the Philippines.

The First Diversion Attack Force was the heart of the failed *Sho-1* plan. Kurita's force began with 32 ships; of these, ten were sunk and three severely damaged. In the aftermath of the battle, the fleet returned to Brunei. On paper, the surviving battleships, *Yamato*, *Nagato*, *Haruna*, and *Kongo*, formed the nucleus of a formidable force. In reality, they were short of fuel and munitions and lacked a proper destroyer screen. Kurita took this force to sea only once during the campaign, and then for only a few days. On November 16, the bulk of this force departed Brunei to return to Japan. Throughout the campaign, this fleet in being gave pause to the Americans who were unaware of its actual condition.

Leyte Gulf marked the end of the IJN's carrier force. Four carriers were sunk in the battle. There were still a few carriers remaining, but there were no trained aviators to fly aircraft off their decks. During the Philippines campaign, Japanese carriers were used for logistical missions to Southeast Asia with limited success. *Junyo* completed a run with shells for Kurita's battleships, but was later torpedoed and damaged after completing a run to Manila. The brand-new fleet carrier *Unryu* was sunk in the East China Sea on December 19 while carrying 30 "Okha" suicide rockets and other cargo bound for Manila. In January, *Ryuho* completed a run to Formosa. The once-mighty Japanese carrier fleet was not a factor in the campaign.

The final force to play a role in the Philippines campaign was Shima's Second Diversionary Attack Force. It began with three cruisers and seven destroyers; of these heavy cruisers *Nachi* and *Ashigara* and five destroyers survived the Battle of Leyte Gulf and remained assigned to the Southwest Area Fleet. Many other surviving warships from the Leyte Gulf battles were sent to Manila to augment Mikawa's Southwest Area Fleet. Destroyers *Hamakaze* and *Kiyoshimo* arrived on October 25 with the survivors of

Following the disaster at the Battle of Leyte Gulf, the IJN had few capable units available for the remainder of the Philippines campaign. One of these was the unique *Shimakaze* shown here running trials in May 1943. The destroyer was an unparalleled torpedo platform being capable of 39 knots and carrying 15 torpedo tubes. However, its capabilities in other areas were inadequate, as was evinced during the campaign. (Naval History and Heritage Command)

The first of the IJN's Number 1-class, first-class transports was commissioned in May 1944. The first ship completed, *Number 1*, is pictured here. Many of the class served in the Philippines and proved very useful with their ability to carry 500 tons of cargo and up to 480 men. (Yamato Museum)

battleship *Musashi*. Destroyers *Hatsuharu* and *Hatsushimo* from Shima's force arrived the same day. The first two returned to Kurita's fleet at Brunei on October 29, but the last two remained under Mikawa's command. Destroyer *Akebono* arrived at Manila on October 26. Two days later, Shima's force reached Manila with its two heavy cruisers and destroyers *Kasumi* and *Ushio*. These were sent to Palawan Island and held in readiness as the "TA Support Force." Heavy cruisers *Kumano* and *Aoba* had been crippled during the Battle of Leyte Gulf and were also in Manila.

By the time Vice Admiral Okochi took over the Southwest Area Fleet, the *TA* operation was ramping up. To protect the convoys going to Leyte, additional ships were sent to Manila. These included the Matsu-class destroyer *Take* on October 30 and fleet destroyers *Asashimo*, *Naganami*, and *Shimakaze* from Brunei the next day. On November 1, the large destroyer *Wakatsuki* and light cruiser *Oyodo* arrived from Japan. A final reinforcement was sent from Kurita at Brunei on November 4 consisting of fleet destroyers *Hamanami*, *Akishimo*, and *Kiyoshimo*. With the exception of *Oyodo* and *Kiyoshimo*, both sent to join Kurita at Brunei, all these ships, totaling two operational cruisers and 12 destroyers, were available for the *TA* operation. This was a considerable force, but the antiaircraft capabilities of Japanese ships, and destroyers in particular, was inadequate to defend against concerted air attack the like of which they would soon face.

As losses mounted during the course of the *TA* operation, the Combined Fleet allocated Escort Squadron 31 to the Southwest Area Fleet on December 5. This was composed of Matsu-class destroyers. Designed to be built quickly and in large numbers, the Matsus were tough ships but were slower and not as well armed as fleet destroyers.

Also coming into service in time for the *TA* operation were new, purpose-built amphibious ships. The T.1-class naval transports were comparable to American destroyer-transports. Based on a Matsu-class hull, these were 1,500-ton ships capable of 22 knots and carrying landing barges which could be launched over the stern even when the ship was underway. The 950-ton T.103 class of landing ships were smaller versions of the USN's LSTs. Though not good sea boats, they were well suited to littoral operations in the Philippines. As part of Transport Squadron 1, both classes of amphibious ships were heavily used during the campaign.

Land-based Air Forces
After the rout of the IJN's surface fleet in the Battle of Leyte Gulf, defense of the Philippines fell to the IJN's land-based air forces. During the Battle

US Intelligence Assessment of Principal Japanese Airfields, September 1944

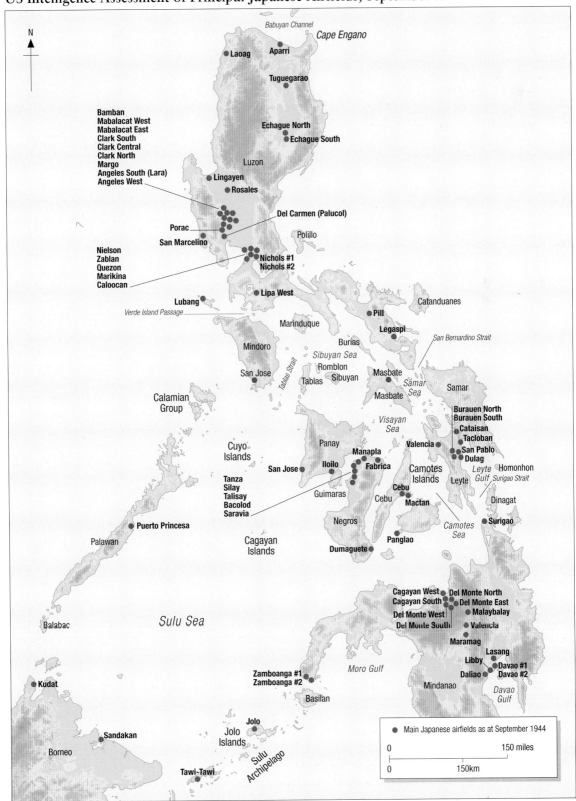

N

Babuyan Channel
Cape Engano

Laoag
Aparri

Tuguegarao

Bamban
Mabalacat West
Mabalacat East
Clark South
Clark Central
Clark North
Margo
Angeles South (Lara)
Angeles West

Echague North
Echague South

Luzon

Lingayen
Rosales

Del Carmen (Palucol)

Porac
San Marcelino

Polillo

Nielson
Zablan
Quezon
Marikina
Caloocan

Nichols #1
Nichols #2

Lubang

Lipa West

Catanduanes

Verde Island Passage

Pill

Legaspi

San Bernardino Strait

Marinduque

Mindoro

Burias

Masbate

Samar

Sibuyan Sea

Romblon

Tablas Strait

San Jose

Tablas Sibuyan

Masbate

Samar
Sea

Calamian
Group

Visayan
Sea

Buruen North
Buruen South

Cataisan
Tacloban

Cuyo
Islands

Panay

Valencia

San Pablo
Dulag

San Jose

Iloilo

Manapla
Fabrica

Camotes
Islands

Leyte
Gulf

Homonhon
Surigao Strait

Tanza
Silay
Talisay
Bacolod
Saravia

Cebu

Leyte

Dinagat

Guimaras

Cebu
Mactan

Puerto Princesa

Negros

Camotes
Sea

Surigao

Palawan

Cagayan
Islands

Panglao

Dumaguete

Balabac

Sulu Sea

Cagayan West
Cagayan South

Del Monte North
Del Monte East

Del Monte West

Malaybalay

Del Monte South

Valencia

Maramag

Lasang

Libby

Davao #1

Kudat

Zamboanga #1
Zamboanga #2

Moro Gulf

Daliao

Davao #2

Basilan

Mindanao

Davao
Gulf

Jolo

Sandakan

Jolo
Islands

Borneo

Sulu
Archipelago

Tawi-Tawi

● Main Japanese airfields as at September 1944

0   150 miles

0   150km

When Onishi formed the first special attack units in the days leading up to their first successful employment on October 25, all the pilots were true volunteers. There was no shortage of volunteers, only a shortage of aircraft. Many of the volunteers were experienced pilots, as in this view showing a lieutenant receiving his orders. (Naval Historical and Heritage Command)

of Leyte Gulf, the First and Second Air Forces were combined into the First Combined Base Air Force. Fukudome was appointed its commander and Onishi became his chief of staff. Its strength fluctuated with the constant expenditure of aircraft in conventional and kamikaze attacks, which extracted very heavy losses, and the stream of reinforcements coming from Formosa. At the start of the campaign, on October 31, the First Combined Base Air Force possessed 273 aircraft, of which 149 were operational.

After the spectacular debut of Onishi's kamikazes on October 25 against the Seventh Fleet's escort carriers off Leyte, more kamikaze units were quickly organized. Though kamikazes represented a small fraction of the First Combined Base Air Force's total sorties during the campaign, they were by far the most effective. To capitalize on the initial success of suicide attacks, Onishi flew to Tokyo in early November to demand the 300 kamikazes he said were required to defeat an American invasion. He came away with only 150 aircraft and pilots from various training centers. Of these, 140 reached Formosa for kamikaze training seven days later.

During November, the IJN tried to keep its land-based air force in the Philippines up to strength. Some 1,000 aircraft were deployed to the Philippines, of which 800 arrived. There was an impressive number of new aircraft, but their pilots were poorly trained with an average of barely 100 hours in the air. The flow of new aircraft during the month meant that replacements exceeded losses by 25 percent. In part to accomplish this, on November 15 the Combined Fleet decided to stop training carrier air groups in favor of reinforcements for the Philippines. For December, another 800 aircraft were allocated to the Philippines, of which 600 arrived. Until mid-December, the total strength of IJN aircraft in the Philippines averaged 600–700 aircraft. After mid-December, replacements failed to keep up with losses. Thus, the First Combined Base Air Force's strength began a steep decline. Japanese sources give the number of aircraft operational on December 15 as 100. By January 1, 1945 its strength stood at 70 or less. The number of replacements in January also fell; of the 120 aircraft allocated, only 100 arrived. Fukudome stated that he had only 47 aircraft left when his command was withdrawn to Formosa on January 8.

Many different IJN aircraft were used as suicide aircraft, depending on what was available. The most numerous IJN kamikaze aircraft was the Mitsubishi A6M "Zeke" single-engined fighter. Its official Allied reporting name was Zeke, but the much more popular name of Zero will be used in this account. By late 1944, the most advanced version of the Zero, the A6M5 with improved performance compared to the A6M2 of early war fame, was totally outclassed by the Hellcat. However, the Zero was well suited to performing as a suicide aircraft, given its fairly high speed and ability to carry a 550-pound bomb. Another early war IJN staple often used as a kamikaze was the D3A2 "Val" dive-bomber. The replacement for the Val was the D4Y "Judy," which was also extensively used in kamikaze missions. Several different types of twin-engined aircraft were assigned to suicide attacks with the most common being the fast P1Y1 "Frances."

The Fourth Air Fleet was the IJA's command responsible for air operations throughout the Philippines. It suffered from the same issues as did its IJN counterpart—very heavy losses and insufficient replacements—and its pilots were no better trained. On October 31, the Fourth Air Army had about 100 operational aircraft. In mid-December, the number of operational aircraft stood at 133.

A kamikaze pilot taxies his bomb-laden Mitsubishi Zero from an airfield somewhere in the Philippines. The Zero could carry a 550-pound bomb; it was the explosion of the bomb that did more damage than the impact of the aircraft. (Naval Historical and Heritage Command)

The Fourth Air Army did not coordinate its actions with the First Combined Base Air Force except in the most general manner. Early in the campaign, per agreement with the IJN, the Fourth Air Army concentrated on attacking American air facilities on Leyte. Later in the campaign it focused on attacking USN forces using suicide tactics. The IJA also saw suicide tactics as the only way to inflict losses on the USN and to possibly stop the invasion of Luzon. The IJA was not as quick to adopt suicide tactics as the IJN, but by November the IJA was organizing 18 special attack units in Japan. The first preplanned suicide attack by the Fourth Air Army was not conducted until November 11 by a special attack unit organized in the Philippines.

The most prevalent IJA aircraft in the campaign, and therefore the aircraft most used in kamikaze attacks, was the Ki-43 "Oscar." It was an obsolescent fighter like the Zero, but was still fast and could carry two bombs, making it a good suicide aircraft. Few American observers could differentiate a Zero from an Oscar, so any small fighter was usually reported to be the more common Zero. Most of the IJA's more modern fighters, like the Ki-61 "Tony" and Ki-84 "Frank," were used for kamikaze escort missions. The Ki-51 "Sonia" light bomber was also widely used as a suicide aircraft. It had a fixed undercarriage so was often reported as a Val by the Americans. The obsolescent Ki-48 "Lily" was used as a kamikaze with little success. The much faster two-engine Ki-45 "Nick" heavy fighter was perhaps the best IJA suicide aircraft.

The IJA was quick to join the IJN in embracing special attack tactics. The Fourth Air Army conducted kamikaze attacks throughout the Philippines campaign with a few notable successes. The most numerous IJA kamikaze aircraft was the Ki-43 Oscar, like that shown here. It had an external similarity to the Zero and shared the same attributes that made it a good suicide aircraft—fairly high speed, agility, and the ability to carry a 550-pound bomb. (Public Domain)

ORDERS OF BATTLE

UNITED STATES NAVY

TASK FORCE 38, LATE OCTOBER 1944

(Vice Admiral Mitscher; relieved by Vice Admiral McCain on
October 30)
**TG 38.1 (Vice Admiral McCain; relieved by Rear Admiral
Montgomery on October 30)**
Fleet carriers: *Wasp, Hornet*
Light carriers: *Monterey, Cowpens*
16 escorts
TG 38.2 (Rear Admiral Bogan)
Fleet carriers: *Hancock, Intrepid*
Light carriers: *Cabot, Independence*
24 escorts including two battleships
TG 38.3 (Rear Admiral Sherman)
Fleet carriers: *Essex, Lexington, Ticonderoga*
Light carriers: *Langley*
22 escorts including four battleships
TG 38.4 (Rear Admiral Davison)
Fleet carriers: *Franklin, Enterprise*
Light carriers: *Belleau Wood, San Jacinto*
13 escorts

TASK FORCE 38, DECEMBER 1, 1944–JANUARY 23, 1945

(Vice Admiral McCain)
TG 38.1 (Rear Admiral Montgomery)
Fleet carriers: *Wasp, Yorktown*
Light carriers: *Cowpens, Monterey*
23 escorts including two battleships
TG 38.2 (Rear Admiral Bogan)
Fleet carriers: *Hancock, Hornet, Lexington*
Light carriers: *Cabot, Independence*
28 escorts including three battleships
TG 38.3 (Rear Admiral Sherman)
Fleet carriers: *Essex, Ticonderoga*
Light carriers: *Langley, San Jacinto*
25 escorts including three battleships

LINGAYEN INVASION FORCE

Task Force 77 (Vice Admiral Kinkaid)
Task Group 77.1 Flagship Group
  Amphibious command ship: one
  Light cruiser: *Boise*
  Destroyers: four
Task Group 77.2 Bombardment and Fire Support Group (Vice
  Admiral Oldendorf)
  Battleships: *California, Colorado, Mississippi, New Mexico,
  Pennsylvania, West Virginia*
  Heavy cruisers: *Australia, Shropshire* (Royal Australian Navy,
  RAN), *Minneapolis, Louisville, Portland*
  Light cruisers: *Columbia*
  Destroyers: 17 (two RAN)
Task Group 77.3 Close Covering Group
  Light cruisers: *Denver, Montpelier, Phoenix*
  Destroyers: six
Task Group 77.4 Escort Carrier Group
  Escort carriers: 18 (each with 23–35 aircraft)
  Destroyers: 20
  Destroyer escorts: seven
Task Group 77.6 Minesweeping and Hydrographic Group
  Various auxiliaries: 69
  Frigates: two (RAN)
Task Group 77.7 Screening Group
  Destroyers: four

Task Group 77.8 Salvage and Rescue Group
  Various auxiliaries: 21
Task Group 77.9 Reinforcement Group
  Amphibious command ship: one
  Transports: 55
  LSTs: 50
  Destroyers: nine
  Destroyer escorts: two
Task Group 77.10 Service Group
  Various auxiliaries: 40 (including 16 oilers)
  Destroyer escorts: six
Task Force 78 San Fabian Attack Force (Vice Admiral Barbey)
  Amphibious command ships: two
  Transports: 29
  Landing Ships, Dock (LSDs): five
  LSTs: 50
  Smaller amphibious craft: 80
  Destroyers: 16
  Destroyer escorts: six
Task Force 79 Lingayen Attack Force (Vice Admiral Wilkinson)
  Amphibious command ships: two
  Transports: 31
  LSDs: four
  LSTs: 38
  Smaller amphibious craft: 104
  Destroyers: 19
  Destroyer escorts: six

IMPERIAL JAPANESE NAVY

December 15 ,1944—only operational ships are included.
First Fleet (Japan)
Battleships: *Yamato, Nagato, Haruna*
Heavy cruiser: *Tone*
Fleet destroyers: five
Southwest Area Fleet
Second Diversionary Attack Force (Lingga)
Battleships: *Hyuga, Ise*
Heavy cruisers: *Ashigara, Haguro*
Light cruiser: *Oyodo*
Fleet destroyers: three
Philippine Forces (most on Luzon)
Escort (Matsu-class) destroyers: five
Submarine chasers: two
PT boats: 19
Midget submarines: ten
Special attack craft: 180
First Combined Base Air Force (mostly at Clark Field)
Operational aircraft: approximately 100
(In addition, the IJA's Fourth Air Army reported 133 operational
  aircraft.)

OPPOSING PLANS

UNITED STATES

The American Plan to Liberate the Philippines

American strategy after the invasion of Leyte was not decided even as the invasion force moved toward Leyte. MacArthur was steadfast in his determination to recapture Luzon after Leyte had been secured. Admiral King advocated a different approach. He wanted to bypass Luzon and land on Formosa while also securing a bridgehead on mainland China at Amoy. This would cut off Japan from her southern resource areas and represented a step closer to Japan itself. King's approach may have been strategically sound, but he lacked the forces to carry it out. Adequate forces to invade Formosa, strongly held by the Japanese, could not be gathered until June 1945. At a conference in San Francisco from September 29 until October 1, 1944, King was convinced of the impossibility of carrying out his Formosa operation and thus grudgingly agreed to the Luzon operation.

Accordingly, the Joint Chiefs of Staff issued a directive on October 3 that Luzon was to be invaded with a target date of December 20. Nimitz was ordered to seize islands on the Bonin group in January and in the Ryukyus on March 1. These were very aggressive timelines and all of them eventually slipped. Nevertheless, MacArthur now had the go-ahead for his long-sought objective of liberating the Philippines.

Even before the landing on Leyte, MacArthur laid out his timeline for subsequent operations. Landings on the intermediate objective of Mindoro Island were scheduled for December 5 with the main landing on Luzon at Lingayen Gulf set for December 20. This timeline was created before the Battle of Leyte Gulf and before it was apparent that the Japanese would make a supreme effort to hold Leyte.

Mindoro Island was well-placed to act as a support base for the invasion of Luzon. Most of the island is mountainous but the Americans believed airfields could be quickly built on the island to cover the Luzon invasion.

All ships coming from Leyte Gulf to Lingayen Gulf had to pass near Mindoro either using the narrow Verde Island Passage to the north of the island or the Mindoro Strait to the south. From northern Mindoro it was less than 100nm to Manila Bay.

The central planning assumption for the December 5 Mindoro invasion was that the AAF based on Leyte would secure control of the air over Leyte and the central Philippines. This failed to occur. In fact, the Japanese achieved

A milestone in MacArthur's campaign to liberate the Philippines was his return to Luzon. In the view, MacArthur and his staff come aboard light cruiser *Boise* on January 5, 1945. Days later, American forces landed on beaches in Lingayen Gulf on Luzon. (Naval Historical and Heritage Command)

local air superiority over Leyte for periods and the scale of kamikaze attacks against shipping inside Leyte Gulf was increasing. Kinkaid realized that the December 5 date was impossible and tried to convince MacArthur that the invasion of Mindoro on this date was too risky. It took him two personal visits to MacArthur, but on the second MacArthur relented and agreed to postpone the Mindoro invasion until December 15 and to move the invasion of Luzon back to January 9, 1945.

Even with the delay, there were still problems with providing the invasion force with adequate air cover. General George Kenney, Commander of Far East Air Forces, admitted that his forces could not provide the required air cover. Much to MacArthur's delight, Kinkaid agreed to pick up the slack by committing his escort carriers to provide direct cover. This was a risky solution since the vulnerable escort carriers would be exposed to air and kamikaze attack from several directions.

MacArthur knew that Mindoro was lightly defended by the Japanese. In fact, the total garrison was fewer than 1,000 men. The area best suited for the construction of airfields was the area of San Jose in the southeast corner of the island. Even though the island was lightly held by the Japanese, the Mindoro invasion was a bold operation with a certain element of risk. It was beyond the range of fighter cover flying from eastern Leyte. The route of the invasion force passed by several Japanese-held islands. The invasion fleet and the airfields to be built at San Jose would be surrounded by Japanese airfields.

Recent experience made it obvious that the principal threat to the invasion force was kamikaze attack. The Americans had yet to devise a method to defeat suicide attacks; for the Mindoro operation much thought was given to increasing the level of air cover to the invasion fleet. Primary air defense coverage was the responsibility of six escort carriers. Additional support was provided by AAF fighters from Leyte. These would augment the escort carrier CAP during the transit and take over total responsibility for coverage at dusk, a favorite kamikaze attack time. TF 38 was also brought in to cover the operation. Halsey agreed to strike airfields on Luzon on December 14–16 and again on December 19–21 if required.

For the invasion of Luzon, the best place to land a large force was at Lingayen. Though most of Luzon is mountainous, there is a large plain stretching from Lingayen Gulf down to Manila, the largest city in the entire Philippines and a major population center. Moving the initial invasion force of four divisions with another in reserve in the face of kamikaze attack required a huge covering force with 18 escort carriers. TF 38 was also tasked to provide indirect support. Only the invasion of Okinawa was larger.

JAPANESE

The American landing on Leyte dictated Japanese thinking about how to defend the Philippines. Both the IJN and IJA decided to make Leyte the scene of the decisive battle for the Philippines. For the IJN, this ended in total disaster. However, through a combination of wishful thinking that the Americans had suffered heavy losses in the Battle of Leyte Gulf and stubbornness to stick to the plan, both services clung to the notion that a decisive battle could still be waged and won on Leyte.

The IJN supported the notion that a decisive battle could be won on Leyte with an all-out effort to move IJA ground forces to the island. On October 28, just days after the battle, both services signed an agreement regarding future air operations. Both agreed to commit a significant portion of their remaining strength and future replacements to the Philippines. The IJN was tasked to interdict American supplies and reinforcements going to Leyte and the IJA agreed to focus on neutralizing American airfields on the island.

Despite the IJN's best efforts to move adequate forces to Leyte and to supply them, the Japanese defense of Leyte was doomed. General Yamashita Tomoyuki, commander of the Fourteenth Area Army in the Philippines, realized this by the first week of November but was ordered by his superior, Field Marshal Terauchi Hisaichi, commander of the Southern Expeditionary Army Group, to keep up the fight on Leyte. This severely constrained Yamashita's options for defending Luzon.

Yamashita had no precise intelligence of American intentions, but he and his staff came up with a remarkably insightful estimate based on American capabilities and operating patterns. The Japanese assessed that Luzon would be invaded between 7 and 10 January, probably at Lingayen Gulf, with a force of ten divisions. Though the estimate of American

A useful amphibious design employed by the Japanese late in the war comprised the landing ships of the Number 103 class. At only 879 tons standard displacement, these were much smaller than American LSTs, and were actually more similar to American LSMs. They could embark 14 light tanks and 120 men or up to 218 tons of cargo. This is *T.146* after being completed in March 1945. (Yamato Museum)

strength was a little high, it was otherwise accurate. The Japanese also expected that an intermediate objective would be seized, but after sending forces to Leyte they lacked the means to defend Mindoro or anywhere else in the central Philippines. After the Americans landed on Mindoro on December 15, Yamashita again requested to his superior that he be able to focus on the defense of Luzon. Instead, Terauchi directed him to counterattack the American position at Mindoro. Not until December 19 was Yamashita ordered to prepare for the defense of Luzon and let the forces on Leyte fend for themselves. Yamashita's defense plan for Luzon was extremely realistic since he knew that he could not successfully defend against an American invasion. He planned to conduct a fighting withdrawal into the mountains of central and northern Luzon and tie up the Americans for as long as possible and inflict as many casualties as possible.

Within this depressing framework, the IJN could add little to the defense of the Philippines. Though a large surface force had survived the Battle of Leyte Gulf and was located at Brunei, it was hamstrung by lack of fuel and munitions. The Combined Fleet's submarine force was too small to defend Luzon or to attack American supply lines supporting the invasion. This left the burden of defense against American invasions at Mindoro or Luzon with the IJN's land-based air forces. Using kamikaze attacks and combined with the IJA's land-based air force, the Japanese assessed any American invasion convoy could be severely attrited before reaching its objective. In reality, following its defeat at the Battle of Leyte Gulf, the IJN had no chance of defending the Philippines and the lack of serious planning in this regard reflected that.

THE CAMPAIGN

TF 38 OPERATIONS, OCTOBER–NOVEMBER 25, 1944

The inability of Kenney's Fifth Air Force to move a significant portion of its strength to Leyte meant that TF 38 was forced to continue operations in direct support of the Leyte invasion. To reduce the threat of Japanese air attacks on Leyte, Halsey maintained an aggressive program of attacking Japanese airfields in the Central Philippines and on Luzon. When it was obvious that the Japanese were making a significant attempt to move troops to Leyte, TF 38 was given an additional task of attacking these heavily guarded convoys. This assortment of missions was undertaken by the four task groups of TF 38, which were exhausted by the high pace of operations since early October 1944. It was also during this period that suicide attacks expanded to striking TF 38 instead of concentrating solely on shipping in Leyte Gulf.

Halsey had to balance the need for providing rest and replenishment to his exhausted task groups while keeping enough strength forward to accomplish the missions described above. After the Battle of Leyte Gulf, task group 38.1 was allowed to steam to the fleet anchorage on Ulithi for a maintenance period. It was joined by TG 38.3 on October 30, but Sherman's task group was only allowed to remain for two days.

The aggressive Halsey was not content to provide CAP to shipping in Leyte Gulf. The flow of Japanese air reinforcements into the Philippines came from Formosa into the area around Manila on Luzon, where the Japanese maintained several large airfields. Halsey ordered his task group commanders to keep constant pressure on the Japanese air facilities around Manila. On October 29, TG 38.2 struck the Manila area.

Bogan's aviators found the airfields full of aircraft. A total of 71 Japanese aircraft were claimed destroyed in the air and another 13 on the ground. In return, 11 American aircraft were lost. Later in the day, Bogan's task group was subjected to the largest kamikaze attack to date. Following the attacks on the Manila airfields, the Japanese assembled 18 kamikazes from seven units to strike back at the American carriers. The CAP was successful in shooting down all but one; however, the last one, a Val, dove on Bogan's flagship, *Intrepid*. Though the aircraft was shredded by antiaircraft fire, it struck the port-side gun gallery. Damage was light, and personnel casualties were limited to ten killed and six wounded.

On October 30, six Zero kamikazes with five escorts were sent to attack TG 38.4 operating east of Samar. Five kamikazes penetrated the CAP to dive against the various carriers in the task group. One hit *Franklin* and caused severe damage, and another hit light carrier *Belleau Wood* and also caused heavy damage. This view shows the result of those attacks, with *Belleau Wood* on the left and *Franklin* on the right. Both ships were forced back to the US for repairs. (Naval Historical and Heritage Command)

The following day, it was TG 38.4's turn to suffer kamikaze attack. An attack group of six kamikazes and five escorts flew from Cebu to strike Davison's task group. Approaching at high altitude, the suicide aircraft eluded the CAP and selected *Franklin* for attack. Three were shot down by antiaircraft fire, but one hit the flight deck creating a large hole and knocking out the aft elevator. The aircraft penetrated to the hangar deck, where its 550-pound bomb exploded. Damage was severe and 33 aircraft were destroyed. In addition, 56 men were killed and 60 were wounded. The damage forced *Franklin* out of action until March 1945. Another kamikaze headed for light carrier *Belleau Wood* after appearing to target *Franklin*. The suicide attacker struck the flight deck abaft the aft elevator. A major fire resulted and engulfed the 11 aircraft spotted aft. These aircraft were destroyed, and 92 crewmen were killed and 97 wounded. *Belleau Wood* was out of the war until February 1945. This was the most destructive suicide attack yet suffered by the fast carriers.

On October 30, all of TF 38 except for TG 38.2 retired to Ulithi. This immediately increased the level of Japanese air attacks on the shipping in Leyte Gulf. Kinkaid also took this opportunity to send most of his ships to Ulithi for a short break. Remaining in Leyte Gulf were three battleships, four cruisers, and 13 destroyers.

This was the peak period of vulnerability for the Seventh Fleet. The Japanese planned a major air onslaught for November 1; the resulting mix of conventional and suicide attacks fell upon TG 77.1 inside Leyte Gulf. Destroyers were the focus of these attacks, with several being damaged and one sunk. The rear-most destroyer in formation was *Claxton*. She was damaged by a Val that just missed the ship, but the explosion of the aircraft's bomb created a large hole on the destroyer's starboard quarter. Another Val hit destroyer *Ammen*. Since the aircraft hit at a low angle, it bounced off the superstructure and damage was light. *Killen* was hit by another Val forward and was further damaged when its bomb scored a near miss. *Bush*, operating in Surigao Strait, was attacked eight times during the morning but skillfully avoided damage. *Abner Read* drew the attention of two more kamikaze Vals. One delivered a mortal blow by dropping its bomb before it crashed; it struck the aft boiler room. The aircraft hit the aft superstructure and caused a large fire. Crewmen were unable to bring the fire under control, which eventually reached the magazine. The resulting explosion caused heavy flooding and a heavy list. At about 1415hrs, just 33 minutes after being struck, the destroyer rolled over and sank. *Abner Read* became the second ship lost to suicide attack.

Following the day's attacks, Kinkaid evaluated the situation in Leyte Gulf as critical. He sent a message to MacArthur to this effect and asked him to request immediate support from TF 38. Halsey received a copy of Kinkaid's message before midnight. He felt he had no alternative but to break off TF 38's replenishment period at Ulithi and move back toward the Philippines. In addition to the serious spate of Japanese air attacks on November 1, Halsey received reports from the Fifth Air Force that a large Japanese force had been spotted in the western Mindanao Sea. Halsey doubted the accuracy of the reports, but they could not be ignored. To reinforce TG 38.2, TG 38.3 was ordered to turn around from its transit to Ulithi and head east toward Leyte. The maintenance period of TG 38.1 was suspended and it was ordered to sortie from Ulithi. Only TG 38.4 was allowed to remain at Ulithi with the damaged *Franklin* and *Belleau Wood*.

In typical fashion, Halsey's solution to the resurgence of Japanese air power over Leyte Gulf was to go on the attack and reduce Japanese air power at its source. He recommended to Nimitz that he take three of his carrier task groups to strike Japanese airfields on Luzon. Halsey felt that three task groups were required to generate the mass required for impactful attacks on Luzon while defending against kamikaze attacks. The start date for the proposed strike was November 5. Nimitz approved this plan on November 2.

The three groups earmarked for the strike on Luzon were east of San Bernardino Strait just before midnight on November 3 when TF 38 ran across *I-41*. The Japanese submarine managed to slam a torpedo into light cruiser *Reno* in TG 38.3. The single torpedo hit the cruiser aft on the port side, affecting power and steering and creating a port list. Sherman ordered that four destroyers provide antisubmarine protection while a fleet tug steamed from Ulithi to take her in tow. The crew successfully fought the flooding and heavy seas from a nearby typhoon and brought their ship back to Ulithi on November 10. Damaging a single ship from Halsey's armada was an insignificant success for the Japanese, but of note is the fact that this was the first time since the Guadalcanal campaign that a Japanese submarine had launched a successful attack against the Fast Carrier Force.

Following its brush with *I-41*, TF 38 continued its transit to launch strikes on November 5. The position selected by McCain was farther off the

Attacks against shipping inside Leyte Gulf was a constant theme of kamikaze operations early in the campaign. On November 1, several destroyers were hit. *Abner Read* was hit by a Val and sank after the fire from the strike reached the ship's aft magazine. This photograph shows the ship on fire; to the left is the probable smoke column from a second Val that was shot down. Note the immense volume of 5-inch shells; even the heaviest antiaircraft fire was no guarantee of stopping a determined kamikaze. (Naval Historical and Heritage Command)

On November 3, TG 38.3 was ambushed by a Japanese submarine. Light cruiser *Reno* was hit by a single torpedo aft. Excellent damage control saved the ship. This is *Reno* two days later with fleet tug *Zuni* alongside. Note the signs of a fire aft, the oil visible to port, and the missing torpedo mount on the starboard side which was pushed overboard to lighten the ship. The submarine responsible for this attack, *I-41*, was sunk by escort carrier aircraft on November 18. (Naval Historical and Heritage Command)

Luzon coast (at least 80nm) than in earlier strikes because he wanted extra sea room to detect and intercept kamikazes. Each of the three task groups were given a specific target area. TG 38.1 was assigned northern Luzon, including the major complex at Clark Airfield, and all shipping located in Lingayen Gulf; TG 38.2, with the smallest number of aircraft, was assigned southern Luzon and the airfields on Mindoro Island; and TG 38.3 was assigned the area around Manila including targets in Manila Bay. As was doctrine for large strikes, a fighter sweep would be followed by successive waves of Helldivers and Avengers. The strength of the attack waves was reduced by McCain's decision to keep more fighters back to reinforce the CAP to counter the kamikaze threat.

At 0615hrs on November 5, TF 38 began two days of strikes. Overall, the Japanese were caught by surprise. The fighter sweep met heavy resistance from interceptors from the major Japanese air bases at Clark and Mabalacat where Hellcats from TG 38.1 claimed 58 Japanese fighters. Strikes against

IJN submarines underperformed during the Philippines campaign. In the period after the Battle of Leyte Gulf, they managed to sink one warship and damage *Reno*. This is fleet submarine *I-45* that sank destroyer escort *Eversole* 60nm east of Dinagat Island on October 29. Another destroyer escort sank *I-45* hours later. (Yamato Museum)

airfields faced extensive Japanese camouflage and dispersal efforts. Nevertheless, total claims for aircraft destroyed in the air and on the ground came to 439.

Strikes against shipping were also successful. Aircraft from TG 38.3 caught heavy cruiser *Nachi* (Shima's flagship) in Manila Bay. Aircraft from *Essex*, *Lexington*, and *Ticonderoga* launched their first strikes against airfields in the Manila area at about 0730hrs. Following these opening strikes, *Nachi* departed the anchorage where she had been camouflaged and headed for the relative safety of open water. Destroyer *Akebono* fell in as an escort.

With Shima stranded ashore, the Japanese ships worked up to 28 knots and prepared for air attack. The Helldivers and Avengers from *Essex*'s Air Group 15 spotted and attacked *Nachi* off Corregidor Island. Between 0730hrs and 1500hrs, the cruiser was subjected to four strikes. The first attack mounted by Air Group 15 claimed three bomb and three torpedo hits. This was an obvious case of overclaiming since when Commander Theodore Winters (commanding officer of *Lexington*'s Air Group 19 and the next strike coordinator) arrived on the scene, he observed *Nachi* still maneuvering at high speed. Accordingly, he ordered his Helldivers and Avengers to attack the cruiser. These claimed four bomb and one torpedo hits. Despite the radical maneuvers of her captain, *Nachi* was struck by a 1,000-pound bomb between 8-inch turrets Two and Three, causing a major fire. In addition, a torpedo hit forward on the starboard side between the bridge and Turret Three. As a result, the forward magazines and the forward engine room were flooded, and the ship was brought to a halt.

By 1400hrs, *Nachi* was able to get underway but only at 7–8 knots. She was attacked in this condition at 1445hrs by Air Group 19 in the final attack of the day. The Helldivers claimed four bomb hits and the Avengers claimed five torpedo hits. Photographic evidence supported the claim of five torpedo hits, all on the port side. The effect was devastating: one torpedo hit forward and blew off the cruiser's bow, which sank at once. Another torpedo hit aft and detonated the aft magazine, which blew off the stern abaft the engine room; the severed stern remained afloat. The other three torpedoes hit the cruiser amidships. No ship this size could withstand such a pounding. At 1450hrs, *Nachi* sank in shallow water some 12nm northeast of Corregidor. In total, *Nachi* was attacked by 80 aircraft before she was blown to pieces in one of the more effective attacks mounted by American naval aircraft against a major IJN fleet unit during the war.

Nachi was caught in Manila Bay on November 5 and subjected to repeated air attacks. In this view, she is dead in the water and smoking. Later air attacks blew the cruiser into three parts and she sank with heavy personnel losses. In the background is destroyer *Akebono* which was strafed and bombed. She was towed back to Manila by destroyer *Ushio*. (Naval Historical and Heritage Command)

In this view, the center section of *Nachi* burns; at right is *Akebono* which the Americans claimed as sunk. The original caption stated: "Destroyer shown skulking in background to pick up cruiser's survivors was mercilessly attacked and left burning and sinking by our planes." A note by the target coordinator added: "We circled down to 20 feet to make sure there were absolutely no survivors. Fifteen or twenty oily figures were served with .50 caliber just to make sure." (Naval Historical and Heritage Command)

Casualties aboard the cruiser were extremely heavy due to the severe pounding and American aircraft strafing the survivors in the water. A total of 807 officers and men were lost with only 220 being saved by two destroyers and a hospital ship dispatched from Manila.

Akebono was strafed by Hellcats from Air Group 15 and was struck by what the Japanese said were two small bombs, setting the destroyer afire. Destroyer *Ushio* arrived to tow the damaged destroyer to Manila. *Ashigara*, the second heavy cruiser in Shima's force, was also present in Manila Bay but escaped attack.

In response, the Japanese mounted an attack with five kamikazes against TF 38 on November 5. A number of Zeros selected TG 38.3 for attack at

The Japanese response to TF 38's November 5 strikes against the Manila area came in the form of five kamikaze Zeros. All but one got through the CAP; two selected *Lexington* for attack. The first was shot down by antiaircraft fire, but the second came in from astern, as seen in this view. Despite being hit by 20mm and 40mm fire, it still managed to drop its bomb and then hit the aft portion of the island. Damage was minimal, but personnel casualties were heavy. (Naval Historical and Heritage Command)

about 1330hrs. Four suicide aircraft eluded the CAP and dove on *Lexington*. Three were shot down by antiaircraft fire but the fourth crashed on the aft portion of the island. The resulting fire killed 50 and wounded 132. The fires were quickly extinguished and the ship was able to continue flight operations.

In addition to the damage to *Lexington*, the two days of strikes cost the Americans 25 aircraft due to combat and another 11 lost to operational causes. In exchange, the Americans accounted for over 400 aircraft and sank *Nachi*. The heavy aircraft losses had the desired effect as the level of Japanese air activity over Leyte in the following days decreased dramatically.

Following the strikes on Luzon, TG 38.2 returned to Ulithi with the damaged *Lexington*. TG 38.4 departed Ulithi and rejoined TGs 38.1 and 38.3 off the Philippines. Since *Wasp* with McCain aboard was sent to Guam to embark a new air group, Sherman took over command of TF 38 until November 13.

THE JAPANESE *TA* OPERATION

Perhaps the most interesting aspect of the entire Philippines naval campaign is how the Japanese reacted to their crushing defeat at the Battle of Leyte Gulf. In essence, they ignored the fact that the IJN had been reduced to mounting only local operations and pressed on with their plan to fight the decisive ground battle on Leyte. To do so, they would have to mount a series of large convoys to move IJA units to Ormoc, the only major port on the western side of Leyte. This was a very risky endeavor given that it would be conducted in the face of American air power. The Guadalcanal campaign provided ample evidence of the futility of moving large numbers of troops without adequate air cover and then keeping them supplied.

The only way to move sufficient forces and heavy equipment to Leyte was by the use of large transports or dedicated amphibious ships. The Japanese designated the operation to move forces to Leyte as *TA* and numbered them sequentially *TA 1* to *TA 9*. These convoys began in Manila and thus had to make a 600nm trek to Ormoc. In addition to the *TA* convoys, the IJA organized the movement of forces from the central and southern Philippines using whatever was available in the way of barges and even sailing ships. These efforts continued throughout the campaign and succeeded in moving at least 6,000 men to Leyte.

The first *TA* operation took place during the Battle of Leyte Gulf. *TA Number 1* (as it was designated after the fact) was focused on moving the 41st Regiment from Cagayan on Mindanao to Ormoc. To accomplish this, Mikawa employed Rear Admiral Sakonju Naomasa's Cruiser Division 16 (composed of heavy cruiser *Aoba*, light cruiser *Kinu*, and destroyer *Uranami*) and five amphibious ships. Since the mission was executed at the height of the Battle of Leyte Gulf, it escaped the full wrath of American airpower. As Sakonju's force approached Manila on the morning of October 23, submarine *Bream* torpedoed *Aoba*. With the heavy cruiser out of action, Sakonju transferred to *Kinu* and resumed the mission on the morning of October 24. Immediately after departing Manila, *Kinu* and *Uranami* were subjected to three hours of air attacks. These caused heavy personnel casualties on both ships but no severe damage, so Sakonju was able to reach Cagayan early on October 25.

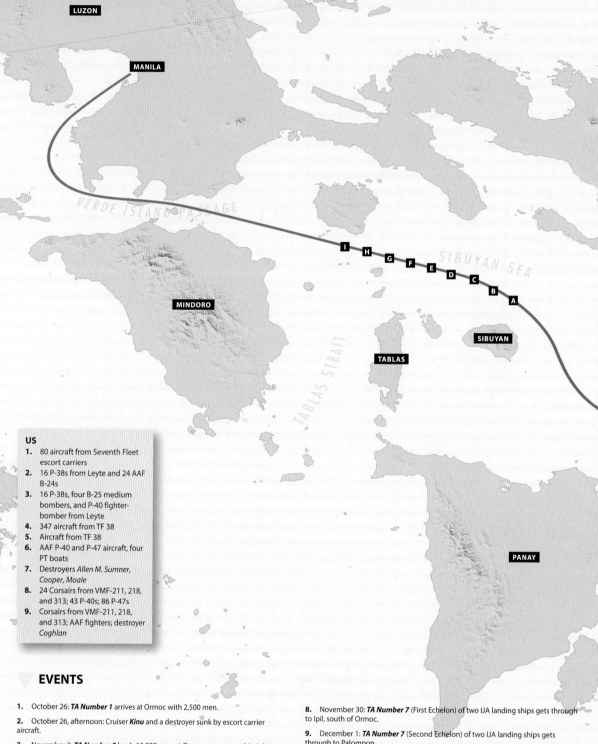

US

1. 80 aircraft from Seventh Fleet escort carriers
2. 16 P-38s from Leyte and 24 AAF B-24s
3. 16 P-38s, four B-25 medium bombers, and P-40 fighter-bomber from Leyte
4. 347 aircraft from TF 38
5. Aircraft from TF 38
6. AAF P-40 and P-47 aircraft, four PT boats
7. Destroyers *Allen M. Sumner, Cooper, Moale*
8. 24 Corsairs from VMF-211, 218, and 313; 43 P-40s; 86 P-47s
9. Corsairs from VMF-211, 218, and 313; AAF fighters; destroyer *Coghlan*

▼ EVENTS

1. October 26: *TA Number 1* arrives at Ormoc with 2,500 men.

2. October 26, afternoon: Cruiser *Kinu* and a destroyer sunk by escort carrier aircraft.

3. November 2: *TA Number 2* lands 10,000 men at Ormoc; one cargo ship is later sunk by B-24 bombers.

4. November 9–10: *TA Number 4* lands almost all of its 10,000 men but with no heavy equipment; two cargo ships and a *kaibokan* are sunk by air attacks.

5. November 11: *TA Number 3* is annihilated by TF 38; four cargo ships, four destroyers, and a minesweeper are sunk.

6. November 24–25: *TA Number 5* fails to reach Ormoc; three landing ships, two transports, and one submarine chaser are sunk by TF 38 air attacks.

7. November 28: The entirety of *TA Number 6* is sunk by PT boats and air attacks; a small amount of supplies is landed at Ormoc.

8. November 30: *TA Number 7* (First Echelon) of two IJA landing ships gets through to Ipil, south of Ormoc.

9. December 1: *TA Number 7* (Second Echelon) of two IJA landing ships gets through to Palompon.

10. December 2: *TA Number 7* (Third Echelon) reaches Ormoc with two landing ships and a transport; destroyer *Kuwa* is sunk by USN destroyers but not before destroyer *Cooper* is sunk.

11. December 7: Continuous air attacks by AAF and Marine fighters sink all four cargo ships and the transport of *TA Number 8*, but most of the 4,000 men aboard reach San Isidro.

12. December 11–12: *TA Number 9* has some success: one cargo ship reaches Palompon and two landing ships land near Ormoc. Following US air attacks and the action of destroyer *Coghlan* near Ormoc, only one destroyer, two submarine chasers, one cargo ship, and one landing ship return to Manila.

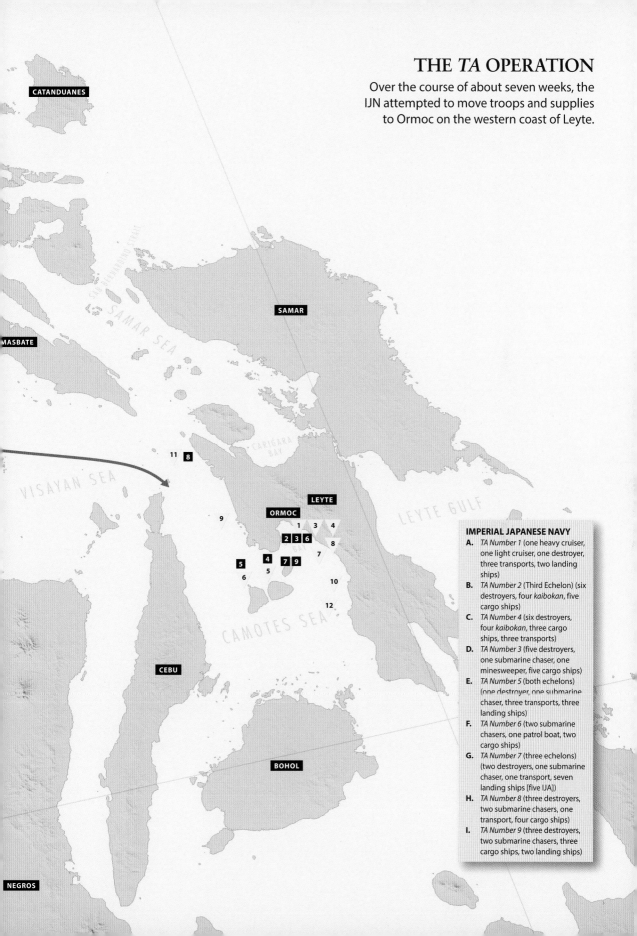

THE *TA* OPERATION

Over the course of about seven weeks, the IJN attempted to move troops and supplies to Ormoc on the western coast of Leyte.

CATANDUANES

SAN BERNARDINO STRAIT

SAMAR

SAMAR SEA

MASBATE

CARIGARA BAY

VISAYAN SEA

11 **8**

LEYTE

9

ORMOC

LEYTE GULF

1 **3** 4

2 **3** **6**

8

7

4 **7** **9**

5

5

6

10

12

CEBU

CAMOTES SEA

BOHOL

NEGROS

IMPERIAL JAPANESE NAVY

A. *TA Number 1* (one heavy cruiser, one light cruiser, one destroyer, three transports, two landing ships)

B. *TA Number 2* (Third Echelon) (six destroyers, four *kaibokan*, five cargo ships)

C. *TA Number 4* (six destroyers, four *kaibokan*, three cargo ships, three transports)

D. *TA Number 3* (five destroyers, one submarine chaser, one minesweeper, five cargo ships)

E. *TA Number 5* (both echelons) (one destroyer, one submarine chaser, three transports, three landing ships)

F. *TA Number 6* (two submarine chasers, one patrol boat, two cargo ships)

G. *TA Number 7* (three echelons) (two destroyers, one submarine chaser, one transport, seven landing ships [five IJA])

H. *TA Number 8* (three destroyers, two submarine chasers, one transport, four cargo ships)

I. *TA Number 9* (three destroyers, two submarine chasers, three cargo ships, two landing ships)

Three transports (*T.6*, *T.9*, *T.10*) and two landing ships (*T.101* and *T.102*) had already departed Cagayan bound for Ormoc. *Kinu* and *Uranami* loaded troops and raced after them. All seven ships arrived at Ormoc on the morning of October 26 where they unloaded 2,500 men from the 41st Regiment. While *Kinu* and *Uranami* were ordered back to Manila to pick up another load, *T.101* and *T.102* were sent to the Visayas for their next load.

On October 26, Sakonju's luck ran out. During the morning, *Kinu* and *Uranami* came under concerted air attack from Seventh Fleet escort carriers in the waters between Masbate and Panay islands. The two ships were overwhelmed by some 80 aircraft; *Uranami* went down around noon and *Kinu* was brought to a stop and sank in the evening. Most of their crews were saved by the three transports which arrived in the area in the mid-afternoon. All three, with Sakonju in command, arrived in Manila the following day. The fate of the two landing ships can be traced briefly. *T.102* was attacked and sunk by escort carrier aircraft in the Guimaras Strait on October 26. *T.101* made it to Bohol Island on October 26 where she embarked an infantry battalion. Surviving an air attack the next day, she delivered about 500 troops to Ormoc. On October 28, *T.101* was sunk by American aircraft in Ormoc.

TA Number 1 successfully delivered some 3,000 troops to Leyte. However, the cost for this success was high—one light cruiser, one destroyer, and two landing ships. This first operation set the pattern for most of those that followed.

The next *TA* operation was the most successful and undoubtedly the most consequential. The main objective of *TA Number 2* was to move the IJA's 1st Division to Leyte. This was an elite unit, and getting it to Leyte would constitute a significant reinforcement of Japanese forces on the island. On October 27, the 1st Division arrived at Manila from Shanghai. The *TA* convoy was planned to carry 10,000 men from the 1st Division. Four fast transports carried the troops—*Noto Maru*, *Kinka Maru*, *Kashii Maru*, and IJA landing craft depot ship *Kozu Maru*. Given the importance of the convoy, the Japanese gave it as strong an escort as possible. Four *kaibokan* (coastal defense ships)—*Okinawa*, *Shimushu*, *CD-11*, and *CD-13*—provided the close escort under Rear Admiral Matsuyama Mitsuji. Rear Admiral Kimura, commander of Destroyer Squadron 1, provided support with fleet destroyers *Kasumi*, *Ushio*, *Akebono*, *Okinami*, *Hatsuharu*, and *Hatsushimo*. Strong fighter protection was provided by IJN fighters from Manila and an IJA fighter regiment flying from bases in the Negros.

The convoy departed Manila at 0740hrs on October 31. Heavy weather covered its transit until the afternoon of November 1 when it was discovered by P-38s flying from Leyte. From 1730hrs to 1820hrs, about ten P-38s attacked the convoy. Japanese fighters were able to protect the transports, and only escort *Shimushu* was strafed. After arrival at Ormoc, unloading of the troops began immediately, but tidal conditions prevented the large transports from using the pier.

By the morning of November 2, most of the troops were safely ashore and unloading of supplies and heavy equipment had begun. Japanese air attacks were directed at the escort carriers in Leyte Gulf to prevent them attacking the convoy, and TF 38 was not in the area. This left the AAF to mount a series of largely ineffective attacks. During the day, 33 P-38s attacked the transports, joined by long-range heavy bombers. The Japanese attempted to defend the convoy with fighters and antiaircraft fire.

In the early afternoon, the Americans made a major effort with 24 B-24 heavy bombers escorted by P-38s. At 1315hrs, *Noto Maru* was struck by a bomb from the B-24s and strafed by P-38s. The ship caught fire; by 1328hrs the captain ordered the crew to abandon ship and the ship sank at about 1500hrs after a large explosion of the ammunition aboard. Before sinking, *Noto Maru* was able to deliver about 3,000 troops and 90 percent of her cargo. *Kozu Maru* unloaded all of her cargo, and *Kinka Maru* 97.5 percent of her cargo. At 1900hrs, the convoy departed and arrived in Manila on November 4. The operation was a major success with 10,000 troops delivered to Leyte, including an entire artillery regiment with 36 guns, and 95 percent of their supplies.

The large convoy was actually the third echelon of *TA Number 2*. The first echelon was landing ship *T.131* which carried an antitank battalion from Manila, arriving at Ormoc on October 30. *T.131* was attacked by B-24s the following day but managed to limp into Manila by November 5. The next echelon comprised transports *T.6*, *T.9*, and *T.10* with 1,000 men of the Imabori Detachment. This small force departed Manila without escort early on October 31 and arrived without loss at Ormoc on November 1. *T.6* and *T.10* returned to Manila while *T.9* transited to Cebu to pick up the headquarters of the IJA's Thirty-Fifth Army. *T.9* arrived back at Ormoc at dawn on November 2.

Following *TA Number 2*, Mikawa was relieved by Okochi. He immediately began planning the next reinforcement operation to Leyte. His Southwest Area Fleet was augmented by additional destroyers and a light cruiser. The large TF 38 strike on Manila on November 5 sank heavy cruiser *Nachi* but the transports and destroyers intended for future *TA* operations were untouched.

The next two *TA* operations were intended to move the IJA's 26th Division to Leyte. *TA Number 3* was planned to take the division's heavy equipment and *TA Number 4* its personnel. The American raid on Manila and a typhoon impeded the loading of the heavy equipment which meant that *TA Number 4* was the first to leave Manila.

Admiral Kimura commanded *TA Number 4* with many of the same ships that participated in *TA Number 2*. The centerpiece of the operation comprised transports *Kinka Maru*, *Takatsu Maru*, and *Kashii Maru* carrying 10,000 men and 3,500 tons of munitions. Also present were *T.6*, *T.9*, and *T.10* with the last 1,000 men of the 1st Division. Close escort was provided by the same four *kaibokan* from *TA Number 2*. Kimura assembled a destroyer screen of six ships—flagship *Kasumi*, *Ushio*, *Akishimo*, *Asashimo*, *Naganami*, and *Wakatsuki*.

TA Number 4 commenced on the morning of November 8 under the cover of bad weather. Proceeding under this fortunate screen, the convoy arrived unmolested in the area of Ormoc in the late afternoon of November 9. Around 1700hrs, AAF aircraft began a series of attacks. The first was conducted by four B-25 medium bombers escorted by 16 P-38s; P-40 fighters assigned to a tactical reconnaissance squadron later joined the assault. The low-level attacks damaged all the cargo ships and all four *kaikoban*, most lightly.

At 1830hrs, the convoy reached the anchorage south of Ormoc. Unloading began at once but was hampered by the fact that a typhoon had destroyed all but ten of the 50 landing barges already delivered to Ormoc.

Take was the second unit of the Matsu class built to replace war losses of fleet destroyers. The Matsu class was an austere design capable of only 28 knots and fitted with three 5-inch guns and a single quadruple bank of torpedo tubes. Like all IJN destroyers, they were incapable of defending against concerted air attack. Take was the victor of the Battle of Ormoc Bay against a USN destroyer force and survived the war. (Yamato Museum)

Three of the *kaibokan* were used to shuttle personnel from the transports to the shore. The unavailability of barges kept much of the cargo on the transports. Just after midnight, the USN tried to disrupt the unloading with four motor-torpedo boats (*PT-524*, *PT-525*, *PT-497*, and *PT-492*). The escorting destroyers fought off the intruders without loss to either side.

The Japanese expected that November 10 would bring heavier air attacks. *Takatsu Maru* and *Kashii Maru* departed at 1030hrs without completing unloading in an effort to avoid air attack. *Kinka Maru* followed at about 1100hrs escorted by two *kaibokan*. Fast transports *T-6*, *T-9*, and *T-10* departed at 1440hrs.

Low-level attacks by 30 B-25s began just before noon. *Kashii Maru* sustained as many as five bomb hits, which caused flooding and a fire. Just after noon, the ship blew up and sank. Most of the crew was saved by a destroyer. *Takatsu Maru* also came under attack from the B-25s.

Hit by at least three bombs, the transport sank instantly. None of the 347 men aboard survived. Three of the *kaikoban* were also attacked. At 1150hrs, *CD-11* was struck by two bombs and lost all power. The ship drifted ashore and was scuttled by gunfire from *CD-13* at 1330hrs. Eighty-nine of her crew were killed.

What remained of the *TA Number 4* convoy split into four groups and was subjected to further air attacks into the early afternoon. At 1410hrs, destroyer *Akishimo* took a bomb forward which broke off her bow and rendered her unnavigable. Minutes later, *Kinka Maru* also took one direct and one near miss.

As the remnants of *TA Number 4* headed back to Manila, they ran into the *TA Number 3* convoy which had departed port on November 9. *TA Number 3* was composed of the cargo ships *Celebes Maru*, *Taizan Maru*, *Mikasa Maru*, *Seiho Maru*, and *Tensho Maru*. These five ships carried 2,000 men and 6,000 tons of equipment and munitions from the 26th Division. The escort for the convoy included destroyers *Shimakaze*, *Hamanani*, *Hatsuharu*, and *Take*, augmented by *Minesweeper No. 30* and *Subchaser No. 46*. In an effort to augment *TA Number 3*'s inadequate screen, Kimura detached *Naganami*, *Asashimo*, and *Wakatsuki* to reinforce the convoy headed east toward Ormoc. After *TA Number 3* detached *Hatsuharu* and *Take* to join Kimura, this left *TA Number 3* with five destroyers.

In fact, the number of destroyers escorting *TA Number 3* was irrelevant. By this point the Americans had realized the significance of the Japanese reinforcement of Leyte. MacArthur had been concerned that the Japanese would reinforce Leyte and extend the battle for the island. Now those concerns were playing out and the AAF units under his command had been unable to stop the flow of Japanese reinforcements. Halsey was about to intervene with TF 38.

Another unknown aspect to the Philippines naval campaign was the movement of the remnants of Kurita's First Diversionary Attack Force to provide distant support for the *TA* operation. On November 9, battleships *Yamato*, *Nagato*, and *Haruna*, heavy cruiser *Tone*, and four destroyers departed Brunei. The task group made a brief move into the Sulu Sea through the Balabac Strait and then returned to Brunei by November 11. Admiral Sherman, in temporary command of TF 38, indicated that Halsey's primary concern in bringing TF 38 closer to the Philippines was to catch Kurita's force had it ventured deeper into the Sulu Sea rather than to attack the next *TA* convoy. In this instance, use of Kurita's force in support of the *TA* convoys was counterproductive since it served to bring Halsey closer to Leyte; once Kurita's force returned to Brunei, TF 38 was able to devote all its attention to *TA Number 3*.

Even before TF 38 intervened, *TA Number 3* had run into trouble. On November 10, *Celebes Maru* ran hard aground on reefs off southern Luzon. The subchaser was detached to guard her until units from *TA Number 4* arrived. The troops aboard were rescued by two *kaibokan*, but no further attempt was made to move them to Ormoc. At sunrise on 11 November, two American PT boats attempted to ambush the convoy southwest of Leyte. The boats were driven off by the escort, but *PT-321* went aground and was lost.

This led to *TA Number 3*'s destruction at the hands of TF 38. Sherman launched a massive 347-aircraft strike from TGs 38.1, 38.3, and 38.4 from their position east of San Bernardino Strait. The strike arrived mid-morning just as the convoy was steaming into Ormoc Bay. With no air cover, and reduced room to maneuver, the result was all but certain. Over the next three hours, the massive strike systematically obliterated the convoy. All four remaining cargo ships were sunk—*Mikasa Maru* with 72 crewmen killed, *Seiho Maru* with 86 crewmen killed, *Tensho Maru* with 76 crewmen killed, and *Taizan Maru* with 65 crewmen dead. American planes strafed the survivors in the water or while wading ashore. As potential combatants on land, they were legitimate targets. Of the 2,000 troops carried on the four transports only about 500 survived. All of the 26th Division's heavy equipment was lost. *Minesweeper Number 30* was also sunk early in the attack.

After the cargo ships were dispatched, follow-on attack waves went after the destroyers now steaming in a column to the west to gain open waters. *Hamanami* led the column followed by *Wakatsuki*, *Shimakaze*, *Naganami*, and *Asashimo*.

Naganami was the first to go under, suffering a huge explosion amidships which broke the destroyer in two. The ship sank rapidly taking 156 men with her; only 72 of her crew survived. *Hamanami* suffered a steering casualty early in the attack so was unable to maneuver to avoid the onslaught of bombs and torpedoes. She sank with the loss of 63 men, but the bulk of the crew (167 men) was rescued when *Asashimo* came alongside.

TF 38 RAVAGES *TA NUMBER 3* (PP. 42–43)

After the Japanese had conducted several successful reinforcement operations for their garrison on Leyte, Halsey moved TF 38 to attack the next convoy. This occurred on November 11 as *TA Number 3* approached Leyte. Halsey launched an overwhelming strike of 347 aircraft against the convoy of four cargo ships escorted by five destroyers and a minesweeper. The carnage began mid-morning as the convoy steamed into Ormoc Bay. All four cargo ships and the minesweeper were sunk first. There were so many aircraft in the target area that some were ordered to orbit until other aircraft completed their attacks.

This scene depicts the final stage of the attack when the five destroyers were steaming west out of the bay. The last two destroyers in the column are visible. *Naganami* (**1**) is the ship on the left. A Helldiver dropped its bomb and missed, but soon the destroyer was hit amidships and broke into two. Hellcats are conducting strafing attacks on the Japanese ships (**2**). Concurrently, a division of Avengers (**3**) is making its attack run from the port beam of the destroyers. The ship on the right is *Asashimo* (**4**), which was the only one of the five destroyers to survive. In the background is one of the four cargo ships (**5**) loaded with troops and supplies for the IJA's 26th Division. The ship is sinking and on fire and will never reach its destination.

Antiaircraft destroyer *Wakatsuki*, a member of the IJN's largest class of destroyers, was also struck early and was unable to maneuver. She was hit by a torpedo amidships and blew up. The unique *Shimakaze*, considered to be a "super destroyer" by the IJN, was the last to sink. She was also hit early but drifted afire until the late afternoon when a magazine explosion ended her misery. Casualties were heavy on the two large destroyers. Only 131 of the combined crews of 600 survived.

Perhaps because she was at the end of the column and was hidden by smoke, *Asashimo* survived the carnage. For the loss of only nine aircraft, TF 38 had virtually annihilated *TA Number 3*. Four cargo ships, four destroyers, and a minesweeper had been sunk.

The Japanese determination to reinforce Leyte underlined the importance of keeping TF 38 in direct support of MacArthur's Philippines campaign. For his part, Halsey was eagerly awaiting the opportunity to strike Japan with his carriers. MacArthur did not want the fight for Leyte to be drawn out by the arrival of more Japanese reinforcements on the island. By November 11, Halsey was forced to concede that his strikes on Japan would have to wait. After crushing *TA Number 3* on November 11, TF 38 withdrew to the east to refuel on the 12th. On November 13, TF 38 again approached Luzon and sent successive attack waves directed at shipping in Manila Bay. The purpose of the strikes was to make it impossible for the Japanese to continue large-scale reinforcement of Leyte by destroying harbor facilities at Manila and sinking the ships the Japanese needed for future large troop movements.

The large strike of over 350 aircraft from nine carriers found a plethora of targets. The largest target present was light cruiser *Kiso* which had arrived only the day before to serve as Kimura's flagship. The Japanese had changed their minds and decided to send the cruiser back to Brunei with Shima and his staff because of the elevated concern of air attacks. Before she could depart, TF 38 aircraft caught her and between 0800hrs and 0923hrs hit the ship with three bombs. One of these was near the boiler room, which caused a loss of power. *Kiso* sank that afternoon some eight miles west of Cavite. Eighty-nine men were lost and 105 wounded, many from the embarked staff.

After demolishing *TA Number 3*, TF 38 struck shipping in Manila Bay. Four destroyers were sunk including *Okinami*. She suffered one direct bomb hit and several near misses and sank upright in shallow water eight miles west of Manila. This is the wreck of the destroyer photographed in 1945. (Naval Historical and Heritage Command)

Four of the nine destroyers present were also sunk. The damaged *Akebono* and *Akishimo* were caught alongside the pier at the old USN Cavite Naval Base. Both suffered direct bomb hits and were set afire. The next day, a large explosion on *Akishimo* further damaged both ships. *Akishimo* rolled over and *Akebono* sank on an even keel. *Akebono* suffered 48 dead and 43 wounded, while *Akishimo*'s crew incurred 15 killed and 25 injured.

Hatsuharu was attacked in shallow water and set ablaze by bombs. The crew fought the fires for ten hours, but the destroyer settled in an upright condition. Most of the crew survived, but 12 died and another 60 were injured. *Okinami* suffered an identical fate with 14 dead and 19 wounded. Seven valuable merchantmen were also sunk or wrecked including *Kinka Maru*, which sank on the 16th after burning for two days.

Following the debacles of November 11 and 13, Okochi suspended the *TA* operation. Kurita ordered the remaining destroyers to leave Manila Bay and head to Brunei. Accordingly, about midnight on the 13th, *Kasumi*, *Asashimo*, *Hatsushimo*, *Ushio*, and *Take* departed Manila Bay. Both Shima and Kimura were aboard.

In spite of the beating received by the IJN, leaving the troops on Leyte without resupply or reinforcement was not an option. Okochi planned a resumption of convoys using a variety of means, but not with convoys of large ships escorted by valuable fleet destroyers. To escort future convoys, he received Escort Squadron 31 comprising expendable Matsu-class destroyers.

The *TA* operation resumed after a two-week break. The next three convoys were originally planned to carry the 68th Brigade to Ormoc with a combination of amphibious ships and small cargo ships. This intention was altered by the immediate need to move supplies to Leyte after the failure of *TA Number 3*. On November 23, *TA Number 5* got underway with landing ships *T.111*, *T.141*, and *T.160*, escorted only by *Subchaser Number 46*, departing Manila. The small convoy reached Port Cataingan on Masbate Island early the next day. TF 38 aircraft found the convoy in the early afternoon and destroyed the landing ships; the subchaser rescued the survivors and headed to Manila.

The second echelon of *TA Number 5* was also a failure. Transports *T.6*, *T.9*, and *T.10* escorted by destroyer *Take* left Manila on November 24 and arrived at Port Balanacan on Marinduque Island the following day. The small convoy was detected by TF 38's morning searches on November 25 and attacked. *T.6* and *T.10* were sunk, and *T.9* and *Take* were damaged but were able to return to Manila. *Subchaser Number 46*, with the survivors of the first echelon convoy, was also detected and sunk.

TA Number 6 employed two small cargo ships, *Shinsho Maru* and *Shinetsu Maru*, with an escort of *Subchasers Number 45* and *Number 53* and *Patrol Boat Number 105* (a salvaged ex-USN ship captured during the Spanish–American War). This convoy departed Manila on November 27, and though subjected to air attacks the following day, reached Ormoc on the evening of November 28. That night, *PT-127* and *PT-331* attacked the convoy with four torpedoes each while it was unloading. These accounted for *Subchaser Number 53* and *Patrol Boat Number 105*. *PT-128* and *PT-191* claimed to have hit the cargo ships' transports as well, but Japanese sources confirm their attack was unsuccessful. The next day, P-40 and P-47 aircraft arrived over Ormoc Bay and forced *Shinsho Maru* ashore. *Shinetsu Maru* and *Subchaser Number 45* departed, but the subchaser was sunk by aircraft later in the day and the cargo ship on November 30. *TA Number 6* did deliver a small amount of critical supplies to the hard-pressed IJA garrison on Leyte but was wiped out in the process.

The next operation consisted of three echelons. The first two featured the IJA's version of landing ships, which were almost identical to the IJN's T.101 class. The first echelon departed Manila on November 28 with *SS.5*, *SS.11*, and *SS.12*, escorted by *Subchaser Number 20*. Heavy weather provided cover. *SS.5* ran aground on Masbate Island, where the convoy stopped to avoid moving during the day. The rest of the tiny flotilla reached a small port just south of Ormoc late on November 30 and unloaded its supplies and 200 men. The following day, all three ships departed for Manila where they arrived safely on December 2, again shielded by heavy weather. The second echelon, comprising *SS.10* and *SS.14*, left Manila on November 30. American air activity prevented them from arriving at Ormoc; instead they diverted to Palompon on northwest Leyte, where they landed their supplies on December 1. Neither returned to Manila.

TA Number 7's third echelon departed Manila on the evening of December 1. This was a convoy of transport *T.9* and landing ships *T.140* and *T.159* with an escort of destroyers *Take* and *Kuwa*. With heavy weather still covering the central Philippines, the convoy avoided air attack and arrived at Ormoc unscathed late on December 2. After unloading, the Japanese encountered a squadron of USN destroyers. *Kuwa* was sunk in this engagement, together with a large American destroyer. The third echelon of *TA Number 7* was a minor success, delivering all its cargo and then defeating a larger American naval force trying to intercept it.

TA Number 8 returned to the notion that a fairly large convoy could reach Ormoc. To move the 4,000 men of the 68th Brigade to Leyte, Admiral Okochi gathered transports *Akagisan Maru*, *Hakuba Maru*, *Shinsei Maru Number 5*, *Nichiyo Maru*, and *T.11*. The escorts consisted of destroyers *Ume*, *Momo*, and *Sugi* (all Matsu-class units) and subchasers *Number 18* and *Number 38*. The convoy departed Manila in the mid-morning of December 5. Progress was unimpeded until the convoy neared Leyte on December 7. At this point

The Seventh Fleet's large force of PT boats was very active during the campaign. They were the first USN units to operate inside Ormoc Bay, where they engaged Japanese barge and reinforcement convoys. PT boats were responsible for sinking two IJN destroyers during the campaign and took part in the successful defense of the Mindoro beachhead in December. In this view, a group of boats are moored near tender *Oyster Bay* in Leyte Gulf in October or November 1944. (Naval Historical and Heritage Command)

the Japanese plan began to fall apart when the convoy commander learned that an American force of 80 ships and craft had just landed south of Ormoc. The Japanese transports were ordered to run aground at San Isidro, 30 miles north of Ormoc.

The convoy was subjected to continuous attacks from waves of aircraft from Leyte, including 24 Corsairs from Marine Fighter squadrons 211, 218, and 313, 86 P-47s, and 43 P-40s. Just as the convoy was entering San Isidro Bay in the morning, the Corsairs attacked at low level. All four transports and *T.11* became total losses. While the vast majority of the 68th Brigade's 4,000 men got ashore, very little of its equipment did. *Ume* and *Sugi* received light damage from air attacks and *Momo* hit a reef that night near Masbate, but all three destroyers and the two subchasers returned to Manila on December 8.

TA Number 9 got underway as the Japanese defense of Leyte was crumbling. Fighting was reported underway for Ormoc itself, so the convoy was ordered to land at Palompon instead. However, once underway, Okochi changed his mind on December 11 and ordered the convoy to head to Ormoc whatever the circumstances. The result was chaos and heavy losses.

Three cargo ships—*Mino Maru*, *Sorachi Maru*, and *Tasmania Maru*—embarked 4,000 men of the Takahashi Detachment while landing ships *T.140* and *T.159* loaded 400 personnel of the Ito Naval Landing Force. The escort was provided by destroyers *Yuzuki*, *Uzuki*, and *Kiri* and subchasers *Number 17* and *Number 37*.

The final *TA* convoy departed Manila on the afternoon of December 9. It was spared air attack on December 10, but the following day the escort commander faced AAF and Marine air attacks in the morning and afternoon as he attempted to carry out Okochi's orders to reach Ormoc. The morning attack was conducted by the three Marine fighter squadrons. Facing a Japanese CAP of some 30 fighters and intense antiaircraft fire, the Corsairs focused on the three transports. Eight Marine Corsairs dive-bombed the largest transport, *Tasmania Maru*, and one of their 1,000-pound bombs left a large hole on the ship's port side. Only two Corsairs were damaged by enemy aircraft and antiaircraft fire.

The afternoon strike took off from Tacloban at about 1530hrs with 42 Marine and AAF aircraft. The Americans commenced their attack as the convoy was 30nm from Leyte. *Mino Maru* was hit and left dead in the water. This left *Sorachi Maru* to head to Palompon under the cover of the subchasers. *T.140* and *T.159* were ordered to continue on to Ormoc escorted by two destroyers.

The two landing ships delivered the Special Naval Landing Force personnel and their amphibious tanks shortly before midnight. American fire from ashore and destroyer *Coghlan* destroyed *T.159*, but *T.140* escaped heavy damage. *Yuzuki* and *Kiri* took *T.140* to the west and headed to Manila.

They were joined by *Sorachi Maru* and the two subchasers. Destroyer *Uzuki* could not join the retreating remnants of the convoy. The veteran destroyer fell victim to a perfect attack executed by *PT-490* and *PT-492*. Using their radars and the dark coast of Leyte as cover, they slowly approached to within 1,000 yards of *Uzuki* and launched six torpedoes. Two of these hit, and the destroyer sank within minutes 50 miles northeast of Cebu Island. Losses were heavy—170 officers and men were lost with only 59 survivors.

On December 12, just after 1500hrs, the survivors of *TA Number 9* were attacked by AAF and Marine aircraft. *Yuzuki* was severely strafed and damaged. Flooding caused the old destroyer to become unnavigable and she sank at 2027hrs 65 miles north-northeast of Cebu with 20 dead. *T.159* was set afire and was later abandoned. *Kiri* was also damaged by strafing. During the afternoon of December 13, *Sorachi Maru*, subchasers *Number 17* and *Number 37*, *Kiri*, and *T.140* arrived at Manila.

This was the last *TA* operation. MacArthur's troops finally seized Ormoc on December 12 after some seven weeks of fighting. The immense effort made by the IJN to support the IJA's fight on Leyte succeeded in prolonging the fight but was totally inadequate to support a successful Japanese counterattack to recapture the island. IJN losses directly attributable to the *TA* convoys were significant, especially at this point of the war with Japanese naval resources quickly shrinking. Combatant losses included one light cruiser, eight destroyers, three subchasers, one *kaibokan*, one minesweeper, and one patrol boat. Shipping losses were even greater, with 16 merchantmen of 73,651 tons, three T.1-type naval transports, and nine landing ships.

Given the disparity in forces in evidence from October to November 1944, Japanese efforts to support the decisive ground battle on Leyte were remarkably successful. Between October 23 and December 11, 1944, nine major convoys were mounted. An estimated 45,000 troops comprising the better part of four divisions were moved to Leyte along with some 10,000 tons of supplies to sustain the fight. This success was due to several factors. The large USN surface forces in Leyte Gulf adopted a defensive approach and only attempted to secure the waters west of Leyte late in the campaign. Remarkably, it is apparent that the Americans did not understand Japanese intentions; after all, it would be reckless to move more troops to Leyte where they could not be supplied. The Americans' biggest problem was their inability to focus air power on the problem. Establishing only periodic air

Uzuki was a member of the 12-ship Mutsuki class of fleet destroyers. She and sister ship *Yuzuki* were assigned to *TA Number 9*. Neither survived the operation. *Uzuki* was attacked by *PT-490* and *PT-492* off Cebu Island. Struck by two torpedoes at about 0100hrs on December 12, the destroyer sank within minutes with the loss of 170 officers and crew. *Yuzuki* was sunk later that day by air attack. (Naval Historical and Heritage Command)

superiority over the waters west of Leyte gave the determined Japanese the opportunity to get their convoys through. Finally, bad weather, predictable in monsoon season, further curtailed the use of American air power.

THE BATTLES FOR ORMOC BAY

The fight on Leyte between two US Army corps and the IJA's Thirty-Fifth Army was as bitter as any during the Pacific War. Despite horrendous weather, the Americans pressed on with their advance and within three weeks of their landing on October 20, 1944 had pinned the Japanese to a narrow area in western Leyte anchored on Ormoc. The flow of reinforcements, aided by the increasingly worsening weather, allowed the Japanese to slow the American advance to a crawl. By December 1, the hard-pressed Thirty-Fifth Army only held a perimeter around Ormoc and the peninsula north of the port. The Japanese had incurred heavy losses and the attacks on the *TA* convoys meant that ammunition and all other types of supplies were in very short supply.

As MacArthur's troops slogged forward, the Seventh Fleet maintained a large force in Leyte Gulf. Since the advance had reached far inland, the combatants inside Leyte Gulf could not provide gunfire support. These ships were kept in the gulf as a deterrent to any potential IJN incursion into the gulf and to provide antiaircraft support to the constantly arriving reinforcement and resupply convoys. This exposed them to constant air attack. CAP proved unable to handle this threat because of the weather and the relatively few numbers of fighters available from the bases on Leyte. Many of the Japanese air attacks were conducted by kamikazes, and these employed increasingly sophisticated tactics.

At around noon on November 27, the Japanese conducted a combined kamikaze-torpedo bomber attack on TG 77.2 with its four battleships, five cruisers, and 16 destroyers. Among the attackers were 11 IJA Ki-43 Oscar kamikazes. The CAP was late in arriving, so the kamikazes were able to select their targets unmolested. Light cruisers *St. Louis* and *Montpelier* and battleship *Colorado* were all struck. Most of the kamikazes selected *St. Louis* for attack. One approached the cruiser from astern (a favorite kamikaze tactic since antiaircraft defenses were lighter from that direction) and crashed on her fantail where her aviation facilities were located, causing a large fire. Five more aircraft missed the ship, one by only a few feet forward. The aircraft's bomb exploded and created enough hull damage and flooding that a port list developed. *St. Louis* was sent back to the US for repairs and did not return to action until March 1945. *Colorado* was attacked by two kamikazes. One hit a 5-inch casemate gun, killing 19 and wounding 72. The battleship remained on station. *Maryland* succeeded in evading a torpedo.

Two days later, the Japanese returned in the form of six Oscar kamikazes. *Maryland* was again selected for attack. A single hit forward caused extensive damage and resulted in the death of 31 men. Two picket destroyers operating in the eastern approaches to the gulf also came under attack from suicide aircraft. *Aulick* was near missed by two, one exploding close enough that extensive topside damage was created, with 31 dead and 64 wounded. The destroyer was forced to return to the US for repairs. *Saufley* received only minor damage.

The Battles for Ormoc Bay

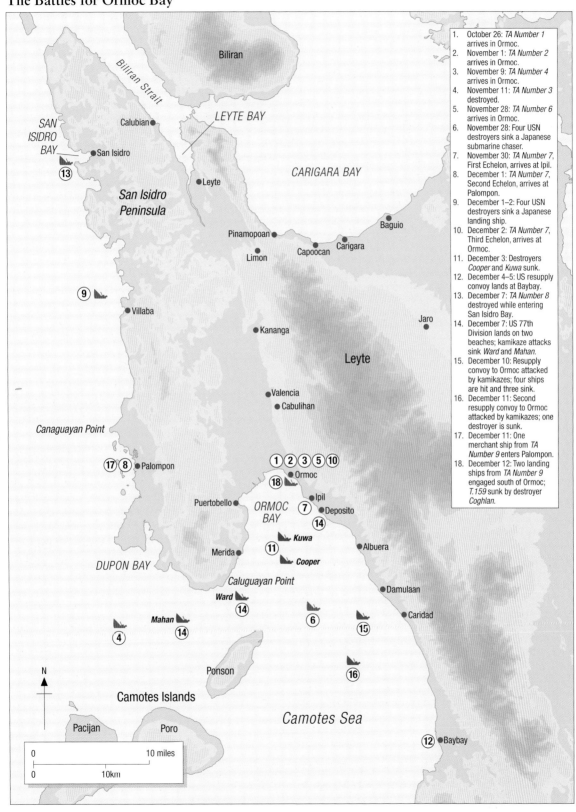

1. October 26: *TA Number 1* arrives in Ormoc.
2. November 1: *TA Number 2* arrives in Ormoc.
3. November 9: *TA Number 4* arrives in Ormoc.
4. November 11: *TA Number 3* destroyed.
5. November 28: *TA Number 6* arrives in Ormoc.
6. November 28: Four USN destroyers sink a Japanese submarine chaser.
7. November 30: *TA Number 7*, First Echelon, arrives at Ipil.
8. December 1: *TA Number 7*, Second Echelon, arrives at Palompon.
9. December 1–2: Four USN destroyers sink a Japanese landing ship.
10. December 2: *TA Number 7*, Third Echelon, arrives at Ormoc.
11. December 3: Destroyers *Cooper* and *Kuwa* sunk.
12. December 4–5: US resupply convoy lands at Baybay.
13. December 7: *TA Number 8* destroyed while entering San Isidro Bay.
14. December 7: US 77th Division lands on two beaches; kamikaze attacks sink *Ward* and *Mahan*.
15. December 10: Resupply convoy to Ormoc attacked by kamikazes; four ships are hit and three sink.
16. December 11: Second resupply convoy to Ormoc attacked by kamikazes; one destroyer is sunk.
17. December 11: One merchant ship from *TA Number 9* enters Palompon.
18. December 12: Two landing ships from *TA Number 9* engaged south of Ormoc; *T.159* sunk by destroyer *Coghlan*.

THE BATTLE OF ORMOC BAY (PP. 52–53)

The IJN's Type 93 torpedoes fitted on cruisers and destroyers played a prominent part in many of the surface actions in the Pacific War. The last time this was true was at the Battle of Ormoc Bay fought on December 2–3, 1944. On this occasion, the Americans sent Destroyer Division 120 into the bay to interdict Japanese shipping. This was composed of three new and inexperienced Allen M. Sumner-class destroyers. Opposing them were two much less powerful IJN Matsu-class small destroyers.

The American destroyers swept into the bay and soon gained radar contact on destroyers *Take* and *Kuwa*. Using their superior gunnery fire control systems, they opened fire. *Kuwa* was sunk and *Take* damaged by 5-inch shells. The Japanese ships returned fire and the American formation fell into disarray, which was

exacerbated as the destroyers clumsily maneuvered to evade potential Japanese torpedoes. This concern was justified since at 0013hrs *Cooper* was struck by a Type 93 fired by *Take*. The ship jackknifed and sank within seconds.

This scene shows the chaos of a night battle. *Cooper* **(1)** has just been hit by a torpedo amidships. In the background, *Kuwa* is aflame **(2)**. Behind her are fires ashore in the area of Ormoc **(3)**. To the left of *Kuwa* is *Take* **(4)**, which is firing 5-inch guns at *Moale* (not shown) and 25mm guns at *Cooper*. The Americans also reported being fired on by Japanese shore batteries and aircraft during the battle. After the loss of *Cooper*, the two surviving American destroyers retreated. *Take* and three amphibious ships survived the battle, which was a tactical victory for the IJN.

Allen M. Sumner-class destroyer *Cooper* took part in USN efforts to clear Ormoc Bay of Japanese shipping. She was sunk by a Japanese destroyer employing Type 93 torpedoes, making her the last American warship lost to this devastating weapon. This is *Cooper c.*March 1944 when she was completed. The wartime censor has deleted the radar antennae on the ship's foremast and Mark 37 Director. (Naval Historical and Heritage Command)

It can certainly be questioned why Kinkaid and MacArthur did not use the Seventh Fleet to execute an amphibious end run to take Ormoc. Insertion of naval forces into Ormoc Bay would also have made it even harder for the Japanese to move troops and supplies into Ormoc. Taking Ormoc or cutting off Japanese convoys to it would have brought the campaign to a quick conclusion since the Thirty-Fifth Army's supply lines were almost entirely dependent on holding the port. Kinkaid's biggest concern was air attack. This seems overblown since the kamikaze threat was already significant and was essentially the same whether the targets were operating in Leyte Gulf or Ormoc Bay. Another reason for caution was the possibility of mines. There are only two ways into the Camotes Sea and Ormoc Bay from Leyte Gulf: the Canigao Channel and the East Canigao Channel. Both are narrow and easily mined.

Perhaps spurred on by the length of the campaign and a desire to bring it to an end, Kinkaid moved minesweepers to clear the East Canigao Channel on November 27 and the Canigao Channel on December 4. Neither channel was mined. On November 28, the first foray by USN combatants other than PT boats into the Camotes Sea was finally made. It was conducted by four destroyers, which shelled a target ashore southeast of Ormoc and then engaged a contact reported by a supporting flying boat. This was probably the 440-ton *Subchaser Number 53* from *TA Number 6*. The second destroyer mission on the night of November 29/30 went deeper into Ormoc Bay. It detected a barge convoy, but it was too far inshore to engage. The next night, November 30, *TA Number 7* unloaded in Ipil southeast of Ormoc.

The third sweep, again conducted by four destroyers, returned to Ormoc Bay on the night of December 1/2. No shipping was discovered in the bay, so the Americans proceeded north along the coast of the San Isidro Peninsula. At about 0224hrs, the destroyers made contact with what was thought to be a Japanese freighter and claimed to have sunk it after 20 minutes of 5-inch gunfire. This was probably *SS.10* or *SS.14* from the second echelon of *TA Number 7*.

The next night, the Americans sent three of the new Allen M. Sumner-class destroyers into Ormoc Bay. *TA Number 7* had been sighted by aircraft on December 2 and a clash was expected. On this moonlit night, Japanese aircraft could track the destroyers' wakes on the smooth surface of the water. They were subjected to several air attacks during their transit from Leyte

Gulf. *Allen M. Sumner* was near missed by a bomb that wounded 11 men, but her combat capability was unimpaired. The three destroyers swept north into Ormoc Bay in a line-abreast formation. Already present in the northern part of the bay were destroyers *Take* and *Kuwa*, providing cover for three amphibious ships. After unloading, the Japanese were preparing to leave Ormoc Bay when *Allen M. Sumner*, *Moale*, and *Cooper* made their appearance. Each of these ships carried six 5-inch guns and ten torpedo tubes compared to the three 5-inch guns and four torpedo tubes aboard the two small Japanese Matsu-class destroyers. The Americans also had the advantage of far superior radar-controlled fire control systems, but the Japanese destroyers carried the redoubtable Type 93 "Long Lance" torpedoes.

A precursor to the invasion of Ormoc was an operation by 11 landing craft and four destroyers to land reinforcements 25 miles south of the port. This convoy came under attack on December 5 from a force of 10 IJAAF aircraft—three Oscars and seven Sonias. Three of the ships were hit. Of these, *LSM-20* sank with the loss of eight crewmen and the wounding of nine more. (Naval Historical and Heritage Command)

Minutes before midnight, *Allen M. Sumner*'s radar picked up the two Japanese destroyers 10nm to the north. Ten minutes later, the Americans opened the engagement with radar-controlled gunnery. *Moale* engaged the lead destroyer *Take* from 7,500 yards, while *Cooper* and *Allen M. Sumner* directed their fire at the trailing *Kuwa* at ranges between 9,000 and 12,000 yards. *Kuwa* was hit by a torrent of 5-inch shells and later sank. As was IJN doctrine, the destroyers returned gunfire and *Take* launched her four Type 93 torpedoes as soon as she could discern a target. One hit *Cooper* amidships at 0013hrs. The Type 93 carried a 1,080-pound warhead, easily enough to sink a destroyer. *Cooper* jackknifed and sank within 30 seconds. Her quick demise took 192 of her crew with her.

This small action was a minor disaster for the USN. Using green ships and crews on a moonlit night was not a recipe for success. The American formation degenerated into chaos once the battle began. In addition to *Cooper*'s loss, *Moale* was hit by three shells and damaged, and both surviving ships were sprayed with shrapnel from near misses. Nevertheless, they had sunk *Kuwa* and damaged *Take* with gunfire. *Take* lost an engine but was still able to withdraw with the three amphibious ships.

This minor defeat did not deter the Americans from planning an amphibious operation to seize Ormoc and bring the campaign to a close. A precursor to the landing at Ormoc was a reinforcement mission from Leyte Gulf to Baybay on the west coast of Leyte located some 25nm south of Ormoc. The reinforcement group comprised eight LSMs and three LCIs escorted by four destroyers. The group arrived at its destination late on December 4 and started to unload. By 0315hrs on December 5, the group had completed unloading and was headed back to Leyte Gulf. After rounding the southern tip of Leyte, the convoy came under attack from eight kamikazes. CAP provided by P-38s and antiaircraft fire took a toll on the attackers, but three got through the defenses. One hit *LSM-20* and sank it; another hit *LSM-23* and caused heavy damage; the last selected destroyer *Drayton* for its attentions. The suicide attacker hit the ship forward and created fires. These were quickly brought under control, but six men were killed.

That afternoon, two more kamikazes arrived to attack the convoy. One hit destroyer *Mugford* and caused severe damage. The kamikaze attacks on December 5, mounted by three Ki-43s and ten Ki-51s, promised that the landing at Ormoc, scheduled for December 7, would receive a hot reception.

THE LANDING AT ORMOC

Despite MacArthur's desire to adhere to the schedule of landing on Mindoro on December 5, this operation was delayed because of the intense level of Japanese air activity. This delay had the side effect of freeing up the amphibious lift and naval support required for an assault on Ormoc. The objective was to land the 77th Infantry Division at Ormoc. Task Group 78.3 was formed to conduct the operation. As was the norm for most Seventh Fleet amphibious assaults, it was composed primarily of small craft. Of the 51 amphibious ships and craft, only four were LSTs; the majority were LCIs. Escort was provided by 12 destroyers. Also included in the operation were a minesweeping unit and an inshore support group.

A sweep by four destroyers into the Camotes Sea commenced the operation on the night of December 6/7. The invasion force departed Leyte Gulf on the afternoon of December 6 and arrived off the designated landing area just south of Ormoc early on December 7. The transit to the invasion area was uneventful and the actual landings went as planned and according to schedule. By 0930hrs, two regimental combat teams from the 77th Division were safely ashore. The defenders ashore had been caught by surprise, but the Japanese reacted quickly with air attacks. The IJN contributed seven Zeros and five Frances suicide aircraft, and the IJA committed nine Oscar kamikazes.

The first, with at least 16 aircraft, roared into Ormoc Bay during the 0900 hour. The P-38 CAP was unable to cope. Four ships, including destroyer *Mahan* and destroyer-transport *Ward*, were deployed as an ASW screen on the western approaches of the bay. Being the largest ship of the four, *Mahan* drew the most attention. In the span of a few minutes, nine aircraft attacked the destroyer. Two or three hit and created fires that could not be contained. The captain ordered his crew to abandon ship just after 1000hrs. At 1150hrs, *Mahan* was scuttled by torpedo and gunfire from another destroyer. Only ten men from her crew were killed or missing.

Three kamikazes focused on *Ward*. In an ironic twist, this veteran ship had fired the first shots of the Pacific War at Pearl Harbor exactly three years before. One of the three aircraft, a Ki-45, struck the ship on the forward port side just above the waterline. The bomber struck with such force that one of the aircraft's engines exited through the other side of the ship. The boiler room being hit, the ship lost all power in only three minutes. The fires caused by the initial explosion could not be controlled and it was quickly apparent that the ship was doomed. Amazingly, nobody was killed. *Ward* was also scuttled by another destroyer.

Following the demise of *Mahan* and *Ward*, Rear Admiral Struble used a short respite to prepare his force for the return transit to Leyte Gulf. The attacks resumed early in the 1100 hour. Destroyer-transport *Liddle* was the

On December 7, the 77th Infantry Division made an amphibious landing just south of Ormoc. This caught the Japanese by surprise, but they quickly recovered with a series of kamikaze attacks from a group of IJA kamikazes—nine Ki-45 Nick twin-engined fighters and five escorting Ki-44 "Tojo" fighters. Three Ki-45s selected fast transport *Ward* for attack, and one hit. This photograph shows the effect of the strike amidships, which started a large fire that could not be controlled. The same group of Ki-45s was also responsible for sinking destroyer *Mahan*. (Naval Historical and Heritage Command)

first to be hit. Her captain was among the 36 killed, but the ship survived.

Another respite followed before the attacks resumed. Destroyer *Lamson* was hit by a kamikaze in her bridge area. The resulting fire consumed the forward part of the ship. When it appeared they could not be controlled and threatened the magazines, preparations were begun to scuttle the ship. Ultimately, this proved unnecessary, and the ship was towed to Leyte Gulf for repairs. Most of the other destroyers in the invasion force were targeted during the course of the 1000-hour attack, but were undamaged. Nevertheless, kamikazes had inflicted a significant toll on the Ormoc Attack Group. One destroyer and a destroyer-transport had been sunk, an LSM had been abandoned after being hit by a suicide aircraft while it was beached, and a second destroyer and a destroyer-transport had been severely damaged.

The landing at Ormoc offered the Japanese a continuing opportunity to launch kamikaze attacks against convoys resupplying the beachhead. These targets were poorly defended. On the day that Ormoc was captured by the 77th Infantry Division, December 10, the kamikaze attacks resumed. On this day, nine IJA aircraft (six Oscars and three Nicks) conducted suicide attacks on shipping in Leyte Gulf. A destroyer, a Liberty ship, a PT boat, and an LCT were hit; only the destroyer survived.

The following day featured both sides running convoys to the western side of Leyte. As detailed earlier, *TA Number 9* was the last Japanese convoy to make its way to Leyte. Under heavy air attack, it landed troops at Palompon on the west coast of Leyte while other ships headed right for Ormoc. In the middle of this desperate Japanese operation, the second American resupply convoy departed Leyte Gulf on the morning of December 11. Escorted by six destroyers, the convoy consisted of eight LSMs and four LCIs.

The first kamikaze attack on the convoy arrived at 1700hrs. Only four fighters were on CAP, and they were unable to cope with 12 kamikazes. Four suicide aircraft selected destroyer *Reid* for attack. Two of these scored direct hits; after the aft magazine exploded, the ship sank in two minutes. Only 152 men, about half her crew, were saved. Destroyer *Caldwell* also came under kamikaze attack, but was undamaged.

No further air attacks developed and the convoy arrived in the area of Ormoc very late on December 11. Before arriving at their destination of Ipil, just south of Ormoc, one destroyer and two LSMs had been detached to unload at a different location farther south. This left four destroyers to protect the remaining ships in the convoy. *TA Number 9* with destroyers *Yuzuki* and *Kiri*, escorting landing ships *T.140* and *T.159*, had already entered Ormoc Bay and was also planning to unload troops near Ormoc. The two landing ships beached and began to unload. *T.159* was engaged by US Army direct and artillery fire. Just before 0200hrs on December 12,

as the remaining Japanese ships were departing, the American destroyers escorting the convoy to Ipil made their appearance. *Coghlan* detected three targets with her radar and opened fire on one using radar from 14,000 yards. The destroyer closed to within 6,000 yards of the target which was never identified visually. At 0213hrs, a larger column of fire was observed and the target disappeared from radar. This marked the end of *T.159*. The remaining three Japanese ships were able to withdraw to the west.

After unloading, the American convoy began to move south at 0400hrs. Friendly CAP appeared at 0700hrs. Nevertheless, all five destroyers were subjected to bombing or kamikaze attacks. *Caldwell* was hit on her bridge by a kamikaze and by two bombs. Thirty-three men were killed and 40 wounded, but the fires from the kamikaze attack were extinguished and the destroyer rejoined the formation.

This was the final air attack on ships supporting the Leyte campaign. The American advance to Mindoro and later Luzon made the last phases of the campaign to clear Leyte a backwater. The last port on the west side of the island, Palompon, was captured on Christmas Day, and the following day MacArthur declared that the island was secure. Aside from the continued operations of PT boats to attack Japanese small boats trying to evacuate troops from the island, naval participation in the Leyte campaign was over. With the fall of Leyte, MacArthur turned his attention to Luzon.

TF 38 OPERATIONS, NOVEMBER 1944

As the battle for Leyte entered its final phase, TF 38 continued its supporting operations. After the two days of strikes against Manila on November 5–6, TF 38 withdrew to the east. TG 38.3 was sent to Ulithi and was replaced by TG 38.2 returning from Ulithi. On November 19, TF 38 returned to Luzon to suppress harbors and anchorages. This was conducted without notable success but over 100 Japanese aircraft were claimed destroyed on the ground.

The lack of targets prompted TF 38 to withdraw the following day. Following an attack on Yap Island, TG 38.4 was sent to Ulithi for long overdue maintenance and replenishment. This left only TG 38.2 and TG 38.3 on station off Leyte with a total of four Essex and three light carriers.

The reduced version of TF 38 headed to Luzon during the night of November 24/25 to strike targets on the 25th. Several targets were found in the area of Dasol Bay on the west coast of Luzon. The largest was the heavy cruiser *Kumano*. She had been initially damaged on October 25 at the Battle off Samar and was further damaged

On November 25, TF 38 conducted a series of strikes against shipping off the west coast of Luzon. The most important target was heavy cruiser *Kumano* which was doggedly trying to return to Japan for repairs. This is a view of the cruiser before *Ticonderoga* aircraft sank her in Dasol Bay. Note the missing bow, which was the result of a submarine attack on November 6. (Naval Historical and Heritage Command)

the next day by aircraft from carrier *Hancock*. The crippled cruiser eventually reached Manila and underwent emergency repairs. On November 4, she departed Manila as part of a convoy bound for Formosa. An American wolfpack of four submarines located the convoy off Luzon and attacked on November 6. Hit by two torpedoes, *Kumano* lost her bow and all power, and was towed to Santa Cruz on the west coast of Luzon. After another round of emergency repairs completed by November 20, *Kumano* again prepared to leave for Japan. Before this could happen, the stubborn cruiser was attacked by Air Group 80 from carrier *Ticonderoga*. Five torpedoes and four 500-pound bombs hit the ship in quick succession. Despite emergency counterflooding, *Kumano* capsized to port with the loss of 398 men.

The 1st Transport Squadron was also operating west of Luzon and was attacked on November 25. Aircraft from *Ticonderoga* and *Langley*, part of Sherman's TG 38.3, spotted three landing ships in the morning. *T.161* was strafed and subjected to several near misses. Minutes later, she was struck

Also caught by TF 38 aircraft west of Luzon on November 25 were ships of the 1st Transport Squadron. Three landing ships (*T.112*, *T.142*, and *T.161*) were sunk. This photograph shows the demise of one of those ships. (Naval Historical and Heritage Command)

by a direct hit amidships and sank. *T.113* and *T.142* were also sunk by air attack at this time. Flagship *Yasojima* was spotted in the afternoon and attacked by Avengers from *Ticonderoga*'s Torpedo Squadron 80. One torpedo hit in the stern was sufficient to sink the 2,448-ton standard displacement ship.

In addition to sinking several valuable ships on November 25, there were signs of increased Japanese air activity over Luzon. With only two groups, there were insufficient fighters to prevent Japanese reconnaissance aircraft from locating TF 38 and to mount a strong CAP from all possible directions. Around noon, the American carriers were preparing to launch their third strike of the day when a large group of Japanese aircraft was detected on radar approaching from the south. TG 38.2 was the first to come under kamikaze attack when, at 1234hrs, a single Zero from a group of six made a dive against *Hancock*. It was destroyed by antiaircraft fire only 300 feet above the ships, but the falling debris inflicted minor damage.

At 1248hrs, another raid of ten to 12 aircraft was detected flying low only 15nm away. CAP had failed to intercept these aircraft, so now it was up to antiaircraft gunners. On this occasion, the kamikazes could not be stopped. One Zero crashed into *Intrepid* at 1253hrs and started a serious fire. Just before 1300hrs, another kamikaze came in from astern. The aircraft hit the flight deck at a shallow angle and broke into pieces casing fires. The bomb aboard the suicide attacker penetrated the flight deck and exploded in the hangar bay. The damage to the flight deck made further flight operations impossible, so the 75 aircraft airborne at the time were forced to recover on other carriers. *Intrepid* was not in danger of sinking but the fires were not brought completely under control until 1447hrs. Casualties to the crew were heavy, with 69 dead and 35 seriously wounded. *Intrepid* was forced to return to the US for repairs, and would not return to action until mid-March 1945.

Other aircraft from the same raid selected *Cabot* for attack. One hit the light carrier on the flight deck forward and another scored a near miss that created hull damage. Damage was severe and 36 men were killed. The light carrier was sent to Ulithi for repairs.

TG 38.3 also came under attack. At 1255hrs, two suicide aircraft dove on *Essex*. One was destroyed by antiaircraft fire, but the second, a Judy, hit the forward part of the flight deck on the port side. Despite an impressive fireball, damage was not serious and flight operations were able to continue. *Essex* was fully repaired in just over two weeks.

Severe damage to *Intrepid* and *Cabot* forced TG 38.2 to withdraw to Ulithi. This left only TG 38.3 on station. In total, kamikaze attacks had inflicted serious damage on fleet carriers *Franklin*, *Intrepid*, and *Essex* as well as light carriers *Cabot* and *Belleau Wood*. Three of these ships were

Escorting the 1st Transport Squadron was *Yasojima*. She was an ex-Nationalist Chinese cruiser built by the Japanese and then sunk in 1937. The hulk was raised and converted into a coast defense ship. This photograph shows the end of *Yasojima*. One of the torpedoes in this view launched from Avengers from *Ticonderoga* hit the ship in the stern, resulting in her loss. Only about 100 of the crew of 340 survived. (Naval Historical and Heritage Command)

The Japanese response to the TF 38 strikes of November 25 focused on TG 38.2. In the second kamikaze attack of the day, two Zeros dove against *Intrepid*. The first was shot down by antiaircraft fire, but the second (shown in the view) survived a Hellcat attack and antiaircraft fire (parts of the Zero can be seen falling off) to execute a skillful dive to hit *Intrepid*'s flight deck. The aircraft penetrated the flight deck and its bomb exploded in the deck below, starting fires on both the flight deck and in the hangar bay. *Intrepid* was struck again minutes later; the cumulative damage forced her to return to the US for repairs. (Naval Historical and Heritage Command)

forced to return to the US for repairs; *Essex* and *Cabot* proceeded to Ulithi for repairs.

Even Halsey was forced to recognize that exposing the TF 38 to suicide attack was foolish, "at least until better defensive techniques were perfected." The efforts of TF 38 after the Battle of Leyte Gulf had a significant operational impact on the effort to liberate the Philippines. It had suppressed Japanese air power and reduced Japanese shipping to levels that were insufficient to move garrisons around the Philippines. Having lost control of the air and without shipping, the Japanese garrisons spread around the Philippines were effectively isolated.

THE INVASION OF MINDORO

With the battle for Leyte in its final stages, MacArthur's next move was to secure Mindoro. The two main elements of the Visayan Attack Force departed Leyte Gulf on December 13. The invasion force was spotted by a Japanese reconnaissance aircraft in the morning, though the first air attacks did not develop until around 1500hrs. The escort carriers and Marine Air Group 12 flying from Leyte maintained a strong continuous CAP over the fleet, but it was not enough.

The first attack was made against Struble's Mindoro Attack Force. *Nashville* was the biggest ship present and a single suicide Oscar selected the light cruiser for attack. Just before 1500hrs, the Oscar skillfully came in at low altitude from astern and stuck *Nashville* on the port side. The bomb aboard the aircraft also exploded. The result was to create immediate and heavy fires in the bridge area. The fire was brought under control but not before 133 men were killed and 190 wounded. *Nashville* had to withdraw to Leyte Gulf with a destroyer escort, and Struble was forced to transfer to a destroyer. Just after 1700hrs, a group of ten aircraft approached the

The American Invasion of Mindoro

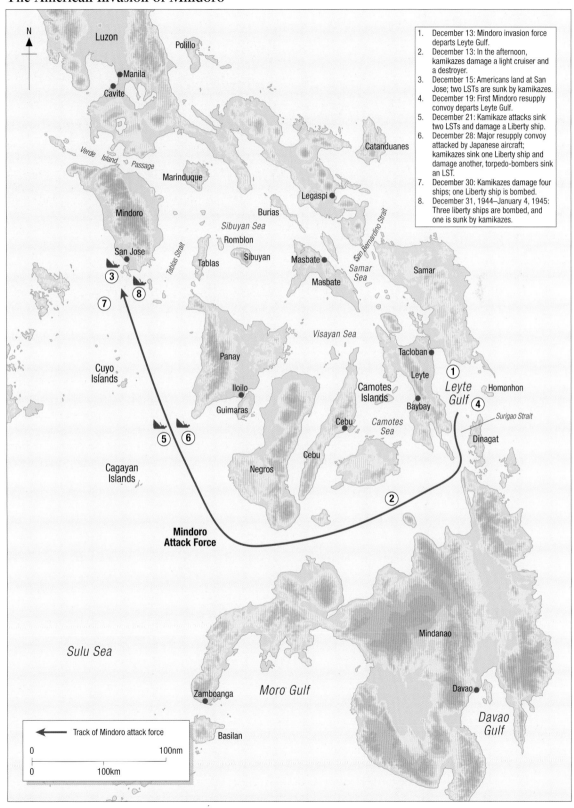

1. December 13: Mindoro invasion force departs Leyte Gulf.
2. December 13: In the afternoon, kamikazes damage a light cruiser and a destroyer.
3. December 15: Americans land at San Jose; two LSTs are sunk by kamikazes.
4. December 19: First Mindoro resupply convoy departs Leyte Gulf.
5. December 21: Kamikaze attacks sink two LSTs and damage a Liberty ship.
6. December 28: Major resupply convoy attacked by Japanese aircraft; kamikazes sink one Liberty ship and damage another, torpedo-bombers sink an LST.
7. December 30: Kamikazes damage four ships; one Liberty ship is bombed.
8. December 31, 1944–January 4, 1945: Three liberty ships are bombed, and one is sunk by kamikazes.

N

Luzon

Polillo

Manila

Cavite

Catanduanes

Verde Island Passage

Marinduque

Legaspi

Mindoro

Burias

Sibuyan Sea

San Jose

Romblon

Sibuyan

Masbate

Samar Sea

Samar

Tablas Strait

Tablas

Masbate

③

⑧

⑦

Visayan Sea

San Bernardino Strait

Tacloban

Cuyo Islands

Panay

Camotes Islands

Leyte

①

Leyte Gulf

Homonhon

④

Iloilo

Baybay

Guimaras

Surigao Strait

⑤ ⑥

Cebu

Camotes Sea

Dinagat

Cagayan Islands

Cebu

Negros

②

Mindoro Attack Force

Mindanao

Sulu Sea

Davao

Zamboanga

Moro Gulf

Davao Gulf

Basilan

← Track of Mindoro attack force

0   100nm

0   100km

The Mindoro invasion force came under kamikaze attack beginning on December 13. The first successful attack was mounted by a single Oscar. The pilot evaded the CAP and dove on light cruiser *Nashville*, flagship of the Mindoro Attack Force. The Oscar hit amidships, where it and the two bombs aboard exploded. This is a view of the affected area after the attack. Damage to the ship was not severe, but personnel casualties were extremely heavy—133 dead and 190 wounded. (Naval Historical and Heritage Command)

escort carrier force. Three suicide attackers survived the CAP and lined up for attacks. Two were dispatched by antiaircraft fire, but the final kamikaze struck destroyer *Haraden* amidships. The crew fought the resulting fires successfully, losing 14 dead and 24 wounded in the process. *Haraden*, too, was forced to return to Leyte Gulf.

The attacks on December 13 were a small taste of what the Japanese had envisioned for the following day. However, there was confusion about where the invasion convoy was headed; the Japanese believed that the American invasion force in the Sulu Sea was headed for either Negros or Panay. Added to this confusion was an effective American program to suppress Japanese airfields. TF 38 handled the Luzon airfields, the escort carriers attacked airfields on Panay and Negros, and the Marine Corsairs from Leyte hit airfields on Masbate and southern Luzon. The effect was to break up any planned large attack. The Mindoro Attack Force was not even spotted and only a few stragglers approached the battleship-escort carrier force before being shot down by the defending CAP.

The first landings at San Jose were recorded at 0731hrs on December 15. They were unopposed, so everything proceeded as planned with the extra benefit of good weather. However, a Japanese reconnaissance aircraft had spotted the invasion force in the morning, which meant an air attack could be expected soon. This developed just after 0800hrs and was directed at the escort carrier group. *Marcus Island* was just missed by a kamikaze that crashed within 20 feet of her starboard bow. Later in the hour, a group of some 20 aircraft came in from the south and headed for the ships off the beach. One suicide attacker struck *LST-738* just above the waterline and penetrated into the tank deck. The resulting fire forced the crew to abandon ship. After burning all day, the LST was scuttled by gunfire. Almost the exact same fate befell *LST-472*. Attacked by four kamikazes, one survived antiaircraft fire and crashed onto the ship. Again, a fire resulted which

On the day of the American landing on Mindoro, the Japanese mustered five groups of special attack aircraft to strike the invasion force off San Jose. The IJN contributed 12 Zeros and a Judy. Five ships were hit, and two were sunk. In this view, *LST-738* burns after taking a kamikaze strike on her starboard side (visible just forward of the "738" on the hull). Destroyer *Moale* stands by to assist. The LST was later scuttled after a series of explosions. The smoke in the left distance may be from *LST-472*, which was also hit and sunk by kamikazes the same day. (Naval Historical and Heritage Command)

could not be contained. *LST-472* was also scuttled by gunfire later in the day.

Spurred on by the threat of additional suicide attacks and aided by ideal beach conditions, the amphibious ships quickly unloaded and departed for the return trip to Leyte Gulf at 1900hrs. The return transit occurred without further incident. The escort carriers were held for an additional day to provide CAP, and then were released on December 16. The first phase of the Mindoro operation had gone extremely well and the first airfield on the island was operational by December 19.

As always, the amphibious phase of an operation was followed by a continual parade of reinforcement and resupply convoys. These offered attractive targets for the Japanese. On December 18, *PT-300* was hit and sunk by a kamikaze. The first resupply convoy for Mindoro brought another large kamikaze response. This large convoy of 14 LSTs and six cargo ships, with an escort of 11 destroyers, departed Leyte Gulf on December 19. On the afternoon of the 21st, it neared its destination and came under air attack. Japanese records indicated that 45 aircraft were committed, of which 15 were lost. In the span of two minutes, five kamikazes, apparently IJA aircraft, broke through the CAP and survived heavy antiaircraft fire to make vertical attack dives. Their aim was deadly—*LST-460*, *LST-749*, and the Liberty ship *Juan de Fuca* were all hit. Another aircraft crashed close to a destroyer, but inflicted little damage.

LST-460 was carrying fuel and ammunition and soon became a blazing wreck. *LST-749* was hit amidships and soon the entire aft section of the ship was ablaze. She was attacked by another group of four twin-engine aircraft; none hit, but the fires gained strength and she was abandoned. Personnel casualties on the two LSTs were high—107 of the 774 sailors and soldiers on the two ships were killed. Damage to the Liberty ship was not serious, and she was able to rejoin the convoy.

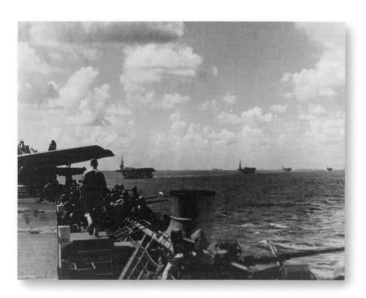

The next chance for the kamikazes came in the final days of 1944, when an even larger resupply and reinforcement convoy of 90 ships and craft escorted by nine destroyers departed Leyte Gulf for Mindoro. Beginning on the morning of December 28, the convoy was subjected to three days of almost around the clock air attacks. CAP was limited to periodic coverage because of bad weather. The first attack by six kamikazes rendered spectacular results. One hit Liberty ship *John Burke*, which was carrying munitions. The ship was engulfed by an explosion and a huge white cloud. After this cleared, there was no sign of the ship and her crew of 68. Another Liberty ship, *William Sharon*, was also hit and a large fire ensued. She was saved by the efforts of the crew of destroyer *Wilson* and was towed back to Leyte Gulf.

That evening, a group of 20–30 Japanese aircraft returned to resume the assault. Attacking in the bright moonlight, a torpedo-bomber hit *LST-750*. The ship was beyond salvage and was scuttled by an escorting destroyer. The attack lasted until after 2000hrs, but no further ships were hit.

A strong CAP from Mindoro saved the convoy from additional loss on December 29 and during the morning of December 30. The convoy commander ordered his charges to unload as quickly as possible so the return transit to Leyte Gulf could begin in daylight with the benefit of air cover. This appeared possible until the appearance of five suicide Vals. Attacking at about 1540hrs, four of the five kamikazes scored direct hits. One hit *Orestes*, an LST converted into a PT boat tender. The ship was set ablaze and was forced to beach near San Jose to avoid sinking. Fifty-nine men were killed and 106 wounded. *Orestes* was later towed to Leyte Gulf and brought back into service.

Another kamikaze struck the aviation fuel tanker *Porcupine*. The initial impact of the suicide aircraft and its bomb killed seven men and created serious fires. These eventually reached the aviation gas and resulted in the constructive loss of the ship.

Two destroyers were also hit. *Pringle* suffered only superficial damage. *Gansevoort*'s damage was much more severe, but by 1640hrs the fires aboard had been extinguished. Without power, the destroyer was towed inshore to an anchorage near the burning *Orestes*. Threatened by fires, the destroyer was towed to another anchorage and abandoned. Boarded by PT boat crewman, she was saved and later returned to service.

The final loss to the convoy was Liberty ship *Hobart Baker*, bombed off the Mindoro beachhead later in the afternoon. The rest of the convoy returned to Leyte Gulf without further incident. The return of the large convoy did not mean that Japanese air attacks on ships supporting the Mindoro operation were at an end. On December 31, 1944 and January 2, 1945, another three Liberty ships were bombed and then forced aground or beached to prevent them from sinking. The last kamikaze attack on the beachhead occurred on the afternoon of January 4. Again, a Liberty ship was targeted, and this ship, *Lewis L. Dyche*, was carrying a full load of munitions. The ship disintegrated with her crew of 71. Only the beginning of the Lingayen invasion made the Japanese finally shift from attacking Mindoro.

Though largely unknown, the Mindoro operation was a template for the invasion of Luzon to follow. Some 200 kamikazes were expended during the Mindoro operation. Japanese air activity impacted the USN's efforts to keep the Mindoro beachhead supplied and resulted in heavy losses. Mindoro proved very valuable as an advanced air base to support the upcoming invasion of Luzon. Two airfields were operational in time to support the movement of the invasion force to Lingayen Bay and a third was completed by January 26. Later, the island proved useful again as a staging point for operations to liberate the southern Philippines.

THE SAN JOSE INTRUSION FORCE

Another forgotten part of the Philippines naval campaign was the penultimate offensive sortie of the Combined Fleet. As was so often the case with IJN planning, the operation to attack the Mindoro beachhead (Operation *Rei*) was ill conceived. At this point in the war the Combined Fleet had little to work with, so the forces committed were inadequate. Given this, there was no way for these forces to generate any kind of impact on American operations. The plan had no real purpose and simply burned fuel and exposed some of the Combined Fleet's few remaining ships to destruction for no gain.

When the Americans landed on Mindoro on December 15, the Japanese intended to send a destroyer force to attack the beachhead, but this plan was scuttled due to lack of fuel. Nine days later, the Combined Fleet was able to gather enough fuel to send a scratch force against the beachhead. This was in support of an Imperial General Headquarters directive to attack the beachhead. The eventual plan to strike Mindoro included a bombardment mission by the Combined Fleet and a raid by IJA forces against the airfields.

The bombardment mission was given by Okochi to Kimura. From his flagship destroyer *Kasumi*, he commanded two new Yugumo-class destroyers

The two most powerful units assigned to the Southwest Area Fleet during the campaign were heavy cruisers *Nachi* and *Ashigara*. *Nachi* was sunk by air attack in early November, but *Ashigara* remained operational and was assigned to participate in the late December unsuccessful raid against the American beachhead at San Jose on Mindoro. This is a prewar view of *Ashigara*. The heavily armed ship carried a main battery of ten 8-inch guns and 16 torpedo tubes. (Naval Historical and Heritage Command)

The San Jose Intrusion Force

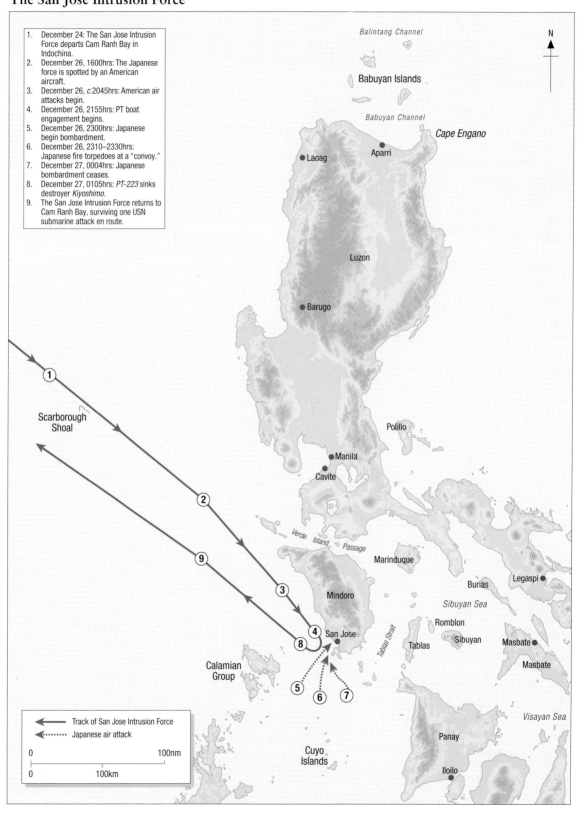

1. December 24: The San Jose Intrusion Force departs Cam Ranh Bay in Indochina.
2. December 26, 1600hrs: The Japanese force is spotted by an American aircraft.
3. December 26, c.2045hrs: American air attacks begin.
4. December 26, 2155hrs: PT boat engagement begins.
5. December 26, 2300hrs: Japanese begin bombardment.
6. December 26, 2310–2330hrs: Japanese fire torpedoes at a "convoy."
7. December 27, 0004hrs: Japanese bombardment ceases.
8. December 27, 0105hrs: PT-223 sinks destroyer Kiyoshimo.
9. The San Jose Intrusion Force returns to Cam Ranh Bay, surviving one USN submarine attack en route.

N

Balintang Channel

Babuyan Islands

Babuyan Channel

Cape Engano

Aparri

Laoag

Luzon

Barugo

Polillo

Manila

Cavite

Scarborough Shoal

Verde Island Passage

Marinduque

Burias

Legaspi

Sibuyan Sea

Mindoro

Romblon

Masbate

Tablas Strait

Tablas

Sibuyan

Masbate

San Jose

Calamian Group

Visayan Sea

Panay

Cuyo Islands

Iloilo

→ Track of San Jose Intrusion Force
◄····· Japanese air attack

0 ————— 100nm
0 ————— 100km

(*Asashimo* and *Kiyoshimo*), three Matsu-class units (*Kashi*, *Kaya*, and *Sugi*), light cruiser *Oyodo*, and the veteran heavy cruiser *Ashigara*. This was a scratch force which had never worked together. The San Jose Intrusion Force was ordered to attack any shipping encountered off the beachhead and then to bombard the airfields and other facilities around San Jose.

In order to have any chance of success, Kimura's force had to achieve surprise. Departing Cam Ranh Bay in Indochina on December 24, it appeared the Japanese would gain just that. Under heavy weather, the San Jose Intrusion Force made it across the South China Sea before being spotted at 1600hrs on December 26 when it was only 180nm from its objective. First detection was made by a Navy B-24 which reported the Japanese force included battleship *Yamato*.

The initial report of an apparently strong Japanese naval force approaching the Mindoro beachhead set off alarm bells at Seventh Fleet. The only naval units in the area of the beachhead were 22 PT boats. Kinkaid quickly organized a group of two heavy cruisers, two light cruisers, and eight destroyers to go to the aid of the beachhead, but this force was in Leyte Gulf and thus had no chance of reaching Mindoro in time. There were a number of Fifth Air Force aircraft based at Mindoro (92 fighters, 13 B-25 medium bombers, and a few P-61 night fighters), but these were unsuited for maritime attack, especially at night. To augment the AAF aircraft, Kinkaid dispatched three Catalina and five Mariner long-range flying boats to attack the Japanese.

The approaching Japanese were next detected by another Navy B-24 some 50nm northwest of the beachhead. Of the 22 PT boats, only nine were suitable for deployment off the beachhead. One of these detected the approaching Japanese on radar at 2048hrs. It took the Japanese until 2155hrs to detect the PT boats and bring them under fire. Not wanting to fall victim to a PT boat trap, Kimura hesitated in his approach, making no progress between 2215hrs and 2240hrs. Meanwhile, the weight of air attacks from the Mindoro-based AAF aircraft and the eight USN flying boats was increasing. Thirteen B-25s, 44 P-38s, 28 P-47s, and 20 P-40s all made attacks, some flying as many as three sorties. *Asashimo* was the target of a near miss that left the destroyer undamaged. *Oyodo* was targeted by B-25s; the cruiser was hit by two 500-pound bombs but one failed to explode and the other did little damage. Much more damaging was the two direct hits on *Kiyoshimo* that left her ablaze and unnavigable. *Ashigara* was hit and damaged by a 500-pound bomb. The strike started a large fire that prompted her captain to order that all the cruiser's torpedoes be jettisoned. Destroyer *Kaya* was damaged when a crashing American aircraft hit her aft stack. The AAF aircraft also strafed the PT boats on the way to attack Kimura's force. *PT-77* was badly damaged by a near miss and had to be escorted back to base at Mangarin Bay.

At about 2300hrs, the Japanese were close enough to the beachhead to start their planned bombardment. The two cruisers fired illumination rounds into Mangarin Bay and soon the Japanese reported sighting a "convoy." *Kasumi* fired four Type 93 torpedoes at this imaginary target at 2310hrs and reported gaining one hit. *Kashi* and *Kaya* fired a total of four more torpedoes, and at 2330hrs the Japanese declared all four hit American transports. The Japanese claimed that the two cruisers and destroyers *Kasumi* and *Asashimo* then followed up with a bombardment of a supply dump from 2345hrs to

Fleet destroyer *Kiyoshimo* was part of the San Jose Intrusion Force. After being crippled by two bomb hits from AAF aircraft during the approach to Mindoro, she was finished off by a torpedo from *PT-223*. Another destroyer saved most of the crew, but 82 men were killed. (Yamato Museum)

0004hrs. The bombardment resulted in hits and a subsequent fire. American records tell a different story of a brief and totally ineffectual bombardment beginning at 2310hrs. The airfield was targeted, but suffered only superficial damage. No personnel were even wounded in the bombardment. *Ashigara* expended over 200 shells in the action.

One success of the bombardment was that Liberty ship *James H. Breasted* was hit by shells and her cargo of fuel set ablaze. Six hundred Army troops were able to disembark without loss. Later examination of the wreck indicated she was the target of aerial bombing, almost certainly from AAF B-25s.

Under constant air attack and with PT boats in the area, Kimura limited the duration of his bombardment. During its retreat, Kimura's force was subjected to more PT boat attacks. *PT-221*'s attack was thwarted by accurate Japanese gunfire, but *PT-223* approached to within 4,000 yards of the crippled *Kiyoshimo* and launched two torpedoes at 0105hrs. One of these struck the destroyer, which sank with the loss of 82 dead and 74 wounded. Most survivors were picked up by *Asashimo*; five later accepted rescue by PT boats. *Asashimo* was subsequently bombed again during the retreat, but suffered no damage. Later that evening, submarine *Baya* encountered Kimura's force on its return transit to Cam Ranh Bay. The captain submerged his boat in advance of the approaching Japanese. Forced to launch his attack using sonar, the salvo of six torpedoes fired at short range all missed. This was the final attack on the San Jose Intrusion Force.

Kimura's raid had accomplished almost nothing except to lose a destroyer and have most other ships in the force damaged to some degree. Despite gaining almost complete surprise, the San Jose Intrusion Force was fought off by a handful of PT boats and aircraft executing difficult night attacks. The San Jose airfield remained in operation, though the Americans did lose 26 aircraft during the frantic efforts to attack the Japanese, most from operational causes. The Combined Fleet's only offensive sortie during the Philippines naval campaign ended in utter failure even though it was directed at a virtually undefended target.

TF 38 OPERATIONS, DECEMBER 10, 1944–JANUARY 10, 1945

From November 25 until December 10, TF 38 was relieved of its responsibility to remain on station off the Philippines. This allowed breathing space to devise better tactics to defeat the kamikaze threat. McCain and his staff came up with several measures. The first was to change the organization of TF 38 from four task groups to three. In part this was done because of carrier damage from kamikaze attack, but more importantly it allowed for the creation of larger task groups which meant more escorts and greater antiaircraft protection.

Several important tactical innovations were introduced. The use of picket destroyers was instituted. These were deployed about 60nm from the task forces along the bearing to the target on days when strike missions were conducted. Early detection was key to defeating the kamikazes since it allowed fighters to be vectored for an interception. Along this line, efforts were made to keep friendly aircraft clear on the most probable kamikaze approach avenue. In that manner, if any approaching aircraft used anything but a standard approach, it was considered hostile. CAP operations were now conducted dawn to dusk with fighters airborne at all altitudes in all four quadrants.

To preclude kamikazes from mixing in with returning American strike aircraft, steps were taken to verify that all returning aircraft were friendly. Returning strike aircraft were required to make a full turn around a picket destroyer so that they could be identified. To deal with any Japanese aircraft trying to masquerade as American, CAP was stationed over the picket destroyers.

Perhaps the most effective innovation was called the "Big Blue Blanket" (USN fighters were painted blue). This required keeping fighters over threat airfields day and night. This tactic had already been tried in part, but TF 38 lacked the numbers of aircraft to implement it in full.

With these new antikamikaze measures, TF 38 resumed operations on December 11 in support of the invasion of Mindoro. By December 13, TF 38 was off the coast of Luzon to commence strike operations against airfields that could threaten the Mindoro landing. The launch point off Luzon was farther north than that used previously so that the Japanese couldn't predict TF 38's operating patterns. Another shift in tactics was the use of the Big Blue Blanket instead of making large strikes on specific airfields. Between December 14 and 16, TF 38 recorded 1,671 offensive sorties, of which 1,427 were conducted by fighters and only 244 by Hellcats or Avengers. This tactic seemed to work, since the Mindoro invasion force was not attacked by Luzon-based aircraft during the period December 14–16. During this period, 27 American aircraft were lost to the Japanese and another 38 to operational causes. Japanese losses were 270 aircraft, mostly on the ground, according to TF 38's claims. In addition to greatly reducing the air threat to the Mindoro invasion force from aircraft based on Luzon, no kamikaze was able to penetrate TF 38's defensive screen.

After this success, TF 38 left its position off northern Luzon for a rendezvous with the fueling group on the morning of December 17. After three days of strikes, the fuel state of many ships, particularly the destroyers, was low. From the start, heavy seas and winds made refueling

The December 18 typhoon that struck the Third Fleet was especially dangerous to TF 38's light carriers. They were converted from light cruisers and had a high center of gravity. *Langley*, shown in this view, reported taking a 70-degree roll. Most of the 146 aircraft lost came from light carriers. (Naval Historical and Heritage Command)

difficult. There were no signs that the storm making refueling so hard would develop into a typhoon, but refueling attempts were ordered halted by Halsey just before 1300hrs. He ordered the Third Fleet to the northwest to attempt refueling the following day. Halsey wanted to stay in the area to finish refueling in order to conduct planned strike missions on December 19 in support of the ongoing Mindoro operation and the upcoming invasion of Luzon. He was willing to take the risk of operating in an area of heavy storms to accomplish the mission.

Halsey changed the refueling point twice more to find fairer seas. Unfortunately for Third Fleet, the last one selected took many of its ships directly into the path of a quick-developing typhoon. By the morning of December 18, the weather had gotten worse. In spite of the best efforts of his staff meteorologists, Halsey did not have a firm idea of the typhoon's location or movement. He ordered the fleet south and to refuel as soon as practicable. The task force commanders tried to comply but refueling was impossible.

Between 1100hrs and 1400hrs, the typhoon reached its full fury. Rain brought visibility down to a few feet. At 1149hrs, the order was given for all ships to take the best course and speed to survive the heavy seas. The heavy ships experienced great discomfort but were not in danger of foundering. In contrast, the destroyers and escort and light carriers faced mortal danger. One light carrier rolled 70 degrees. Total aircraft losses from the fleet—all from the light carriers, the escort carriers of the replenishment group, and the floatplanes from the cruisers and battleships—totaled 146.

Destroyers faced the greatest peril. Many were already low on fuel, making their stability even more questionable in heavy seas. Destroyer *Hull* recovered from several 70-degree rolls. But when combined with a 110-knot wind gust, she ended up on her beam ends and began flooding. Only 62 of 264 aboard survived when she went under. *Monaghan* was the next destroyer to succumb. She lost power and foundered after several heavy rolls. Only six men from her crew survived. The last destroyer lost was *Spence*. As a Fletcher-class destroyer, she was more stable then the two other older destroyers that had already gone down, but she was down to 15 percent of her fuel capacity. She began to water ballast too late. At 1110hrs, she went under after two severe rolls. From her crew of about 330, only 24 survived. Several other destroyers survived rolls of 70 degrees or more because of good ship handling, jettisoning top weight, and taking on seawater ballast in their fuel tanks.

At 1500hrs on December 18, the weather began to moderate. Rescue efforts continued into the following day for the survivors from the three destroyers that had gone down. Third Fleet's encounter with the typhoon was equal to a defeat in battle. Three destroyers, 790 men, and 146 aircraft were lost. Following the disaster, a court of inquiry was formed at Ulithi. Its finding after examining the evidence and interviewing over 50 witnesses

Of course, the smaller ships suffered the most in the typhoon. Here, light cruiser *Santa Fe* rolls about 35 degrees to starboard as she rides out a typhoon. The forward 6-inch/47 gun turret is trained to port to avoid shipping water through its gun ports. If a 10,000-ton cruiser was taking these kinds of rolls, it is easy to imagine what the destroyers were suffering. (Naval Historical and Heritage Command)

was that Halsey was responsible for the incident. Throughout the storm he failed to communicate with his task force commanders to seek their advice, and reduced McCain to the status of an observer. Halsey clearly prioritized maintaining TF 38's refueling and strike schedule over the safety of his fleet. The court found him negligent and guilty of errors in judgment as he attempted to meet his mission requirements. Nimitz concurred with the court's findings with only slight alteration.

Having been bashed by the typhoon, Third Fleet spent December 19 reorganizing and refueling. The planned strikes on Luzon on December 21 were scrubbed by bad weather. As a result, TF 38 headed to Ulithi for repair and replenishment. Repairs were completed by December 29, and on the following day TF 38 sortied.

Halsey had finally secured Nimitz's permission for the first USN carrier sweep into the South China Sea. But first TF 38 was tasked to reduce Japanese air power in the region preparatory to the landing on Luzon. Strikes against Formosa were planned on January 3 and 4, followed by a day for refueling, then a day of strikes on Luzon on January 6. Depending on the situation, January 7 would be devoted to more strikes on Luzon or Formosa. Fueling was planned on the 8th and then more strikes on Formosa to cut the flow of air reinforcements to Luzon. The landing at Lingayen Gulf was scheduled for January 9. If everything went according to plan, TF 38 would be unleashed to proceed into the South China Sea after the Luzon landings.

Once again TF 38 gained complete surprise when it began its next series of strikes. Early on January 3, McCain's carriers began launching from a point 140nm off Formosa. Each of the three task groups was given a target area. All of Formosa was covered, as was the Pescadores in the Formosa Strait and Okinawa. The Big Blue Blanket tactic was employed to suppress kamikaze attacks.

Weather sharply curtailed the effectiveness of McCain's strikes on both days. The results of the strikes were difficult to assess, though Formosa-based aircraft were unable to participate in attacks against the Luzon invasion force for the first week. Bad weather also served to protect TF 38 from air attack.

On January 6, the attack shifted to airfields on Luzon. Once again the weather was a problem. Japanese losses were relatively minor and formation of the Big Blue Blanket was impaired by weather so it failed to suppress kamikaze attacks against the invasion fleet. Because of the incomplete work done on the 6th, Oldendorf requested that Luzon be struck again on January 7. Early in the day the weather had improved, allowing blanket tactics to be used over most of the Luzon airfields until 2100hrs. During the day Japanese air activity was light and only four aircraft were claimed by American aviators in the air. Added to this was another 75 claimed destroyed on the ground. In return, 28 aircraft from TF 38 were lost, most due to operational causes. The efforts of TF 38 and the 11 escort carriers providing direct air cover was successful in reducing Japanese attacks against the Luzon invasion force on January 7 to a minimum.

On January 8, TF 38 refueled. On January 9, the day of the grand invasion on Luzon, TF 38 again targeted airfields on Formosa and the Ryukyus. Bad weather was again a factor so the 717 offensive sorties failed to make a big impact. For their part, the Japanese elected to conserve aircraft. Very few aircraft were sent aloft and those on the ground were protected with heavy dispersal and extensive use of decoys.

During the week of January 3–9, TF 38 flew 3,030 offensive sorties, dropping some 700 tons of bombs. American losses reached 86 aircraft, 40 of them to operational causes. This level of support directly impacted the intensity of Japanese attacks on the Luzon invasion force.

THE INVASION OF LUZON

The American invasion of Luzon was one of the largest amphibious operations of the war. From 16 different bases, the invasion force carrying four divisions, with another in reserve, began to assemble in December 1944. Kinkaid was in overall command with Oldendorf overseeing the operations of the escort force.

In addition to the antikamikaze measures taken by TF 38, the Americans tried to mount as heavy a CAP as possible over the invasion force. The escort carriers kept an average of 40 fighters airborne and this was augmented by AAF aircraft. At times the total CAP amounted to 68 aircraft. In spite of these efforts, kamikazes were still able to get through and conduct attacks. One of the biggest problems was providing adequate early warning of approaching threats. Proximity to the many islands near the route of the invasion force degraded radar performance.

A warm-up to a week of unrelenting kamikaze attacks came on January 3. Only a small number of IJN kamikazes were launched this day; despite the heavy CAP, a suicide attacker broke through and crashed 500 yards astern of escort carrier *Makin Island*. The first damage inflicted by the Japanese did not come until the afternoon of January 4 as the invasion fleet was almost ready to depart the Sulu Sea. A single twin-engined bomber, probably an IJA Ki-45 Nick, evaded radar detection and was not spotted until it was diving on escort carrier *Ommaney Bay*. The bomber hit the ship's island and then the flight deck before smashing into the sea. Both bombs aboard the aircraft exploded and caused massive damage. One penetrated into the hangar deck and started a major fire while the second penetrated even further into the forward engine room. Loss of power made fighting the fires on the hangar deck being fed by refueled and rearmed aircraft impossible. *Ommaney*

The most serious blow against the USN during the Philippines campaign was scored by kamikazes on January 4, 1945. On this date, the escort carrier group was caught by surprise by a single kamikaze. In a perfect attack, the suicide aircraft, probably a Ki-45 Nick, landed a bomb on *Ommaney Bay* before hitting her amidships. The resulting fires forced the crew to abandon ship. Minutes later, the aft magazine exploded, as seen in this view. (Naval Historical and Heritage Command)

Bay was abandoned an hour after the kamikaze hit and was scuttled by a destroyer. She was the second escort carrier lost to suicide attack. Casualties aboard the carrier totaled 93 killed and 65 wounded.

Worse was to come on the following day, January 5. By this point Oldendorf's fleet was transiting north along the southwestern coast of Luzon, only about 150nm from the major Japanese airfields. Now certain the Americans were headed for Lingayen Gulf, the Japanese made a major effort to disrupt the landing. A group of kamikazes was intercepted in the morning and another around noon. None of the kamikazes broke through to conduct attacks.

Both the IJN and IJA committed special attack forces to attack shipping inside Lingayen Gulf on January 5, 1945. A number of ships were hit, including heavy cruiser *Louisville* seen here. The fireball from the crash of a Judy looks devastating, but damage to the ship was not severe. Kamikazes lacked the hitting power to inflict heavy damage to armored warships like a heavy cruiser, but they could cause extensive topside damage and heavy personnel casualties. (Naval Historical and Heritage Command)

THE DEATH OF *OMMANEY BAY* (PP. 76–77)

On January 4, 1945, the escort carrier group providing air cover for the Luzon invasion force came under attack. Throughout the day the CAP performed well, defeating several large raids sent from Japanese air bases on Luzon. Remarkably, a single twin-engined bomber evaded the radar from all of the ships in the task force and was not even sighted until it began an attack dive on *Ommaney Bay*.

At 1712hrs, the kamikaze approached the escort carrier from dead ahead and began strafing. Only one ship, *New Mexico*, opened fire before the aircraft hit the ship. Aiming for the bridge, the kamikaze struck it with a glancing blow and hit the flight deck; it went over the side and caused little damage. However, the two bombs aboard the aircraft were dropped before the aircraft crashed, and these were perfectly placed. One penetrated to the hangar deck and exploded among all the aircraft there, which were in the process of being dearmed and defueled. A huge fire caught hold of the forward hangar bay. The second bomb penetrated to the forward boiler room where it exploded. Damage-control efforts were hampered by poor communications and the fires grew unchecked. The crew was forced to abandon ship one hour after the kamikaze strike and the carrier was later scuttled.

In this view the kamikaze (**1**), a Ki-45 Nick bomber, is about to strike *Ommaney Bay* (**2**). Battleship *New Mexico* (not shown) is directing a few rounds of 20mm fire at the suicide aircraft before it strikes the carrier. Note that the aircraft has just dropped two bombs (**3**) which will strike the ship in critical areas and create mortal damage.

The most versatile strike aircraft on USN carriers was the Grumman TBM Avenger, which could perform torpedo attack and conventional bombing missions. This is an Avenger aboard *Wasp* being loaded with a Mark XIII torpedo on October 13, 1944 before a Formosa raid. Chances to employ torpedoes during the Philippines campaign were comparatively few; most Avenger sorties were flown against land targets. (Naval Historical and Heritage Command)

The third wave of kamikazes came in during the late afternoon, breaking through the CAP. From the total of nine IJA suicide aircraft launched that day, a Ki-43 hit the number two turret of heavy cruiser *Louisville*. The resulting fires were quickly brought under control. The Australian destroyer *Arunta* also suffered the attentions of a single kamikaze but survived with only a near miss.

The escort carriers came under heavy attack from a group of 15 IJN kamikazes and two escorts, all Zeros. Coming in at very low altitude, two Zeros selected escort carrier *Manila Bay* for treatment. After popping up to 800 feet for its attack dive, the first hit the flight deck in the area of the island and penetrated to the hangar deck. The resulting fire from the kamikaze strike and its exploding bomb was quickly brought under control. The cost was still high—22 dead and 56 wounded. Escort carrier *Savo Island* avoided a direct hit through the adroit maneuvering of her captain and the accuracy of her antiaircraft crews. Four Zeros headed for escort carrier *Tulagi*, but three were shot down by antiaircraft fire. The fourth veered away to hit the destroyer escort *Stafford* and created a large hole which flooded the engine room. The ship was forced to return to the US for repairs. Nearby Australian heavy cruiser *Australia* was also hit by a Zero. Damage to the ship was light, but the explosion of the aircraft's bomb killed 25 men and wounded 30.

The last attack of the day, probably by IJA Ki-51 light bombers, focused on the minesweeping group. Of the four suicide aircraft, only one found a target—*LCI(G)-70*. The small craft survived being hit but lost two dead.

Before the deadly late-afternoon kamikaze attack, two Matsu-class destroyers were spotted by American aircraft attempting to escape from Manila Bay. The nearest Allied ships were in the minesweeping group. Fletcher-class destroyer *Bennion* and two Australian ships were vectored to intercept. The American destroyer gained radar contact at 1548hrs and opened fire with her 5-inch guns from 23,500 yards. Once intercepted, the Japanese changed course back to Manila Bay and laid smoke to cover their

The heaviest day of kamikaze attacks delivered against Lingayen invasion force was January 6. Both the IJN and IJA contributed aircraft for a total of 44 kamikazes. Light cruiser *Columbia* had the dubious distinction of being hit by both an IJN and an IJA aircraft on the same day. A Zero hit her first, followed by another strike at 1734hrs, as shown here. The aircraft is a Ki-51 Sonia as evinced by its fixed landing gear. (Naval Historical and Heritage Command)

escape. *Bennion* closed the range to 14,300 yards but was unable to score a hit on the retreating Japanese. After firing 349 rounds, *Bennion* broke off the chase. By this time, the escort carriers were able to launch a strike of 16 Avengers and 19 fighters. *Momi* was hit by a torpedo from one of the Avengers. She blew up and sank with all hands. *Hinoki* was also struck by a torpedo and suffered moderate damage. Though 21 of her crew were killed and 45 wounded, she was able to return to Manila.

To complete her saga, two days later *Hinoki* tried again to depart from Manila Bay after undergoing temporary repairs. In the outer approaches to Manila Bay, she encountered part of the American invasion force flowing north to Lingayen Gulf. This time, *Hinoki* ran into four American destroyers led by *Charles F. Ausburne*. The American ship gained radar contact at a very impressive 40,000 yards at 2115hrs. By 2226hrs, *Charles F. Ausburne* had closed to within 10,000 yards and fired illumination rounds to light up the target. Once spotted, *Hinoki* fired torpedoes at her tormentor, but these missed. Meanwhile, *Charles F. Ausburne* was engaging the Japanese ship with full broadsides. At 2235hrs, hits were observed and *Hinoki*'s speed was seen to drop. In the final phase, the American destroyer closed to within 1,100 yards to finish off *Hinoki*. She sank with all hands. The Americans suffered no damage.

As the invasion force began operations in Lingayen Gulf, kamikaze attacks grew to a crescendo on January 6. In total, the Japanese sent 44 kamikazes in three waves, interspersed with conventional attacks. After a small attack in the morning that caused no damage, kamikaze activity picked up just before noon. One suicide attacker struck the bridge of battleship *New Mexico*. Thirty were killed, including her commanding officer and a British lieutenant general assigned to MacArthur's staff. Destroyer *Walke* was attacked by four kamikazes. Three were hit by antiaircraft fire, but one struck the destroyer's bridge, killing her captain.

The new *Allen M. Sumner* was also hit by a single kamikaze. Fourteen men were killed and another 29 wounded.

The only ship to be sunk on January 6 was destroyer-minesweeper *Long*, which was attacked by two Zeros. Hit initially at 1215hrs, she was hit a second time in the afternoon and sank the following day. Another converted four-stacker destroyer, *Brooks*, was crashed into by a single Zero just after noon. She was towed back to the US, but upon arrival was declared a total constructive loss. Another group of kamikazes arrived during the 1700 hour to resume the carnage. *California* was in the process of retiring for the night when she was struck by a single kamikaze. Heavy personnel casualties resulted, some from indiscriminate antiaircraft fire from other American ships. Forty-five men were killed and 151 wounded. Kamikazes lacked the penetrating power to cripple heavily armored battleships, but they could cause extensive topside damage, including to exposed antiaircraft gun crews. *California* and *New Mexico* both remained on station.

Light cruiser *Columbia* was hit on her main deck by a Zero and the aircraft penetrated two more decks before the bomb aboard exploded. Prompt flooding of the aft magazines may have saved the ship. At 1729hrs, the ship was hit again, this time by a Ki-51. Despite her damage and the loss of her two aft 6-inch gun turrets, the cruiser remained on station to complete her naval gunfire support duties. Heavy cruiser *Minneapolis* suffered light damage. *Louisville* was hit for the second day in a row, this time by a Judy. With her bridge heavily damaged, she was forced to leave the battle area for repairs. *Australia*, quickly becoming a suicide magnet, was also hit for the second time in consecutive days. Though she suffered 14 more dead and another 26 wounded, she remained in the fight.

The minesweeping group came in for more attention. Destroyer *O'Brien* was hit on her fantail. Destroyer-minesweeper *Southard* was also struck, but her damage-control parties extinguished the resulting fires within 30 minutes.

January 6 was one of the bloodiest days of the war to date for the USN. Twelve ships had been hit, with personnel casualties totaling 167 dead and over 500 wounded. This level of damage was unsustainable. Oldendorf warned Kinkaid that if the troop transports were exposed to the same level of attack a great slaughter could ensue. He requested that Japanese airfields on Luzon be suppressed by TF 38.

This carnage had been inflicted by the Japanese with a fairly low level of investment. Sources differ, but the number of kamikaze aircraft committed during the day were as low as 44 and as high as 58. On January 6, the escort carriers had been overwhelmed. They lacked adequate numbers of fighters to maintain a strong CAP; the usual amount of 24 fighters airborne at once was not enough. Another problem was the fighter itself. The Wildcats flown from the escort carriers lacked the speed, maneuverability, and rate of climb to deal with the Zero. Fighter direction was also an issue since the nearby land features played havoc with ships' radars.

A much-needed respite from the kamikazes was forthcoming on January 7. That did not mean that Oldendorf's force received no damage. The poorly protected minesweeper group continued to attract more than its fair share of attention. Around 0430hrs, a couple of torpedo planes conducted a night attack. One was seen to be destroyed by antiaircraft fire, but before it crashed, it launched a torpedo at destroyer-minesweeper *Hovey*. The ship was hit and sank in three minutes. At around dusk, the

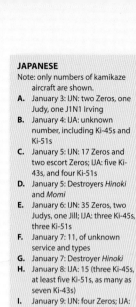

JAPANESE

Note: only numbers of kamikaze aircraft are shown.

A. January 3: IJN: two Zeros, one Judy, one J1N1 Irving
B. January 4: IJA: unknown number, including Ki-45s and Ki-51s
C. January 5: IJN: 17 Zeros and two escort Zeros; IJA: five Ki-43s, and four Ki-51s
D. January 5: Destroyers *Hinoki* and *Momi*
E. January 6: IJN: 35 Zeros, two Judys, one Jill; IJA: three Ki-45s, three Ki-51s
F. January 7: 11, of unknown service and types
G. January 7: Destroyer *Hinoki*
H. January 8: IJA: 15 (three Ki-45s, at least five Ki-51s, as many as seven Ki-43s)
I. January 9: IJN: four Zeros; IJA: two Ki-43s
J. January 10: 70 IJA suicide boats
K. January 10: IJN: at least one Ki-67 Peggy; IJA: five Ki-43s
L. January 12: IJA: 30 (at least one Ki-51, one Ki-67, five Ki-48s, and two Ki-45s)
M. January 13: IJA: two Ki-84 Frank

US NAVY

1. TG 77.6 and TG 77.7: 75 ships and craft, mostly minesweepers
2. TG 77.2: six battleships, five heavy cruisers, one light cruiser, 17 destroyers
3. TG 77.4: 18 escort carriers, 20 destroyers, seven destroyer escorts
4. TG 77.3: three light cruisers, six destroyers
5. TG 77.9: 116 ships, mostly transports and LSTs
6. TF 78: 188 ships and craft, mostly amphibious
7. TF 79: 204 ships and craft, mostly amphibious

EVENTS

1. January 3: First kamikaze attacks.
2. January 4: IJA kamikazes sink escort carrier **Ommaney Bay**.
3. January 5: Combined IJN/IJA kamikaze force damage escort carrier **Manila Bay** and four other ships.
4. January 5: Destroyers **Momi** and **Hinoki** run into TG 77.6; **Momi** later sunk by TG 77.4 aircraft.
5. January 6: Massive kamikaze attack hits 12 ships including two battleships and four cruisers; one destroyer-minesweeper is sunk.
6. January 7: No ships are hit by kamikazes, but two destroyer-minesweepers are sunk by conventional air attack.
7. January 7: **Hinoki** sunk by four USN destroyers.

8. January 8: 15 IJA kamikazes damage five ships including escort carriers **Kadashan Bay** and **Kitkun Bay**.
9. January 9: Four divisions land at two locations in Lingayen Gulf.
10. January 9: Small-scale kamikaze attacks damage three ships, including two cruisers.
11. January 10: 70 IJA suicide boats hit nine ships and craft inside Lingayen Gulf, but only one LCI is sunk.
12. January 10: Small-scale IJA kamikaze attack damages two ships.
13. January 12: Last large kamikaze attack damages eight ships.
14. January 13: Final kamikaze attacks damage two ships, including escort carrier **Salamaua**.

THE ORDEAL OF THE LINGAYEN INVASION FORCE

The Invasion of Lingayen Gulf took place between January 6 and 9, 1945. The Allied force was led by Admiral Jesse Oldendorf. After a three-day bombardment by USN and RAN warships, on January 9 US Sixth Army units landed between the towns of Lingayen and San Fabian.

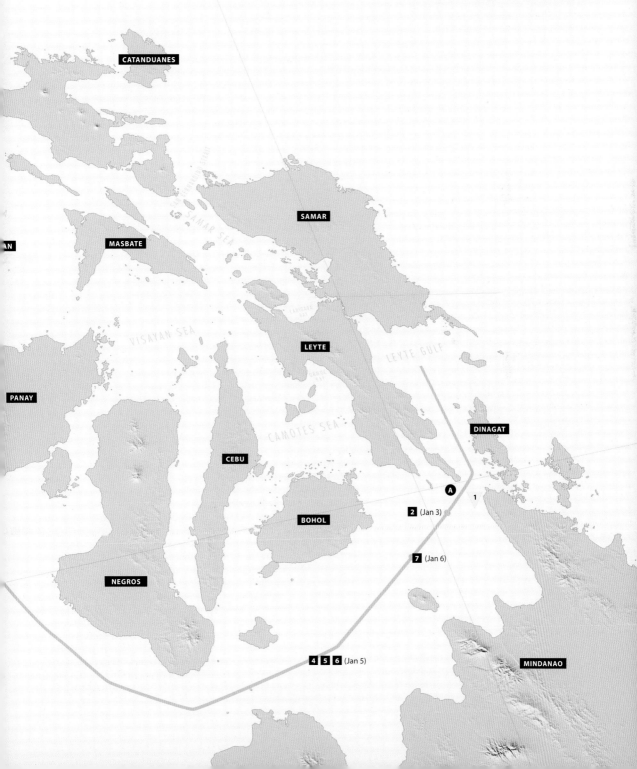

CATANDUANES

SAMAR

MASBATE

N

SAMAR SEA

VISAYAN SEA

LEYTE

LEYTE GULF

PANAY

CAMOTES SEA

DINAGAT

CEBU

A

1

2 (Jan 3)

BOHOL

7 (Jan 6)

NEGROS

4 5 6 (Jan 5)

MINDANAO

A column led by battleship *Pennsylvania* enters Lingayen Gulf on January 7 to begin preinvasion bombardment of Japanese defenses. Behind *Pennsylvania* are battleship *Colorado*, heavy cruisers *Louisville* and *Portland*, and light cruiser *Columbia*. (Naval Historical and Heritage Command)

Japanese paid another visit to the minesweepers. This time, destroyer-minesweeper *Palmer* was struck by two bombs. She sank within six minutes with a loss of 28 dead and 38 wounded.

On January 8, the IJA assumed the burden of kamikaze attacks. *Australia* was attacked in the morning and was damaged again. A Ki-45 was shot down short of the cruiser, but the aircraft's wreckage crashed close aboard and hit the ship's hull. Another was shot down by antiaircraft fire, but this time when the wreckage hit the ship, one of its bombs exploded, creating a large hole in the hull. An LST and an attack transport were also damaged, but otherwise the vital troop transport groups were not attacked. Most of the suicide aircraft went after the escort carriers. An Oscar from a large group of some 20 aircraft hit *Kadashan Bay* at her waterline creating a large hole, but the bombs aboard the aircraft failed to explode thus limiting damage.

In this amazing combat action photograph, an Oscar approaches escort carrier *Kadashan Bay* shortly after daybreak on January 8 while west of Luzon supporting the Lingayen operation. In spite of the visible tracers from 20mm guns and 5-inch bursts, the kamikaze (trailing smoke) hit the carrier on its starboard side at the waterline. The resulting damage forced *Kadashan Bay* to return to the US for repairs. (Naval Historical and Heritage Command)

Even so the carrier was ordered back to Leyte Gulf for repairs and was out of action until mid-April. A group of six kamikazes went after *Kitkun Bay*. Four of them were shot down by CAP, but another Oscar crashed the ship at the waterline on the port side, causing extensive flooding and a loss of power. The carrier was saved by the damage-control efforts of her crew, but was forced out of combat for months with a loss of 16 dead and 37 wounded.

By now, the Japanese were simply running out of aircraft, and the flow of air reinforcements to the Philippines had been stopped. Nevertheless, the invasion fleet was subjected to five more days of spasmodic attacks. On January 9, two destroyer escorts were damaged and light cruiser *Columbia* was hit for the third time. The damage caused was severe and she was ordered to retreat for repairs with another 24 dead and 68 wounded. *Australia* was also hit again, this time by an Oscar, and finally forced to exit the battle to seek repairs. Two kamikazes selected *Mississippi* for attack. One struck a glancing blow; structural damage was light, but the bloody toll of personnel was 23 killed and 63 wounded.

All the action of the preceding week was in preparation for the landings on January 9. The morning landings at two different points went extremely well. With a single exception, the Japanese elected not to defend the beaches, and the veteran American staffs and ships developed a good landing plan and carried it out efficiently.

On the night of January 9/10, the Japanese introduced another suicide weapon: suicide boats operated by the IJA. Each carried two 260-pound depth charges with a crew of two or three. The regiment operating these craft had 70 boats available. At about 0200hrs on January 10, these sortied from a small port on the right flank of the American landing area. Usually entering the target area at slow speed, the boats approached their targets from the stern and when alongside dropped a depth charge at a shallow setting.

After a week of suicide attacks, the landings in Lingayen Gulf went off in near flawless fashion on January 9. On the left is the flagship of Vice Admiral Barbey's TF 78, the command ship *Blue Ridge*. Attack transport *Thuban* is to the right. (Naval Historical and Heritage Command)

Using this simple tactic, nine ships were hit. Only one, *LCI(M)-974*, was sunk. One transport incurred a 12-foot hole below the waterline that caused flooding. Two LSTs were also holed, but survived, too. Two other LSTs suffered lesser damage. Another LCI was badly damaged. Many of the 70 suicide boats were engaged by gunfire during the attack and presumably sunk. Precise Japanese losses are impossible to determine, but by the morning the special attack regiment was no longer capable of operations.

In the days following the landing, kamikaze attacks—all by the IJA—began to wither away. Destroyer escort *LeRay Wilson* was hit on January 10 by a glancing blow, but was still badly damaged. An Oscar struck attack transport *DuPage* loaded with troops—32 were killed and 157 wounded.

The final day of massed kamikaze attacks during the campaign was January 12. The IJN had expended all available aircraft, but the IJA mustered 30 aircraft for suicide attacks. In the morning, destroyer escort *Gilligan* was clipped by a twin-engined aircraft; a second destroyer escort was riddled by shrapnel from a near miss after coming to *Gilligan*'s aid. High-speed transport *Belknap* was attacked by single-engined aircraft. Only one got through, but when it crashed amidships, it created serious damage, killing 38 and wounding 49. The ship was never repaired. Merchant ships in the reinforcement convoy also came under attack, with five suffering hits; aboard the Liberty ship *Kyle V. Johnson*, 128 Army troops and a sailor were killed.

The final attacks were recorded on January 13. Only two suicide aircraft were dispatched, both IJA Ki-84 Franks. One surprised the crew of escort carrier *Salamaua*. Unengaged by antiaircraft fire, the Frank hit amidships. One of the aircraft's bombs exploded on the hangar deck and the second passed through the ship creating a hole near the waterline. The carrier was left without power while major fires took hold. Damage control was ultimately successful, but not before 15 were killed and 88 wounded. *Salamaua* was out of the war until April. Also on this day, attack transport *Zeilin* was hit by a probable IJN aircraft conducting an impromptu suicide attack.

HALSEY'S RAMPAGE

Halsey's desire to execute a grand raid by his Third Fleet into the South China Sea was rejected by Nimitz in November. On December 28, as the invasion of Luzon loomed, Nimitz assented to Halsey's plan.

The operation began on the night of January 9/10. TF 38 entered the South China Sea through the Luzon Strait, followed by the refueling group. Bad weather prevented a planned refueling from taking place on January 10. However, by noon of the following day, TF 38 was fully fueled and was ready to execute Halsey's plan. Intelligence indicated that hybrid battleship-carriers *Ise* and *Hyuga* were located in Cam Ranh Bay. To attack them, Bogan's TG 38.2 would divide into two parts and head toward Cam Ranh. One part included the group's three fleet and one light carrier and the second was built around two battleships. The surface group was ordered to conduct a bombardment of Cam Ranh and finish off any Japanese ships damaged by the airstrikes. The other two task groups were positioned behind Bogan's.

In addition to the three main carrier task groups, TG 38.5 was created for night operations with night-capable carriers *Enterprise* and *Independence*. On January 12, aircraft from these carriers were launched to conduct a predawn search of Cam Ranh and surrounding bays looking for targets. Nothing was found. The intelligence indicating the presence of the two Japanese battleships was wrong; in fact, they had departed for Lingga two weeks earlier. This news notwithstanding, all three carrier groups launched their strikes at 0730hrs while the surface action group closed on Cam Ranh.

Though Halsey had failed to find his primary target, what TF 38 did find off the coast of Indochina was much more valuable to the Japanese. American aviators searched some 420nm along the coast and found an abundance of shipping. Throughout the day, TF 38 flew 984 strike missions, almost all of them directed at shipping. The result was the largest number of ships sunk by airstrikes on a single day during the war.

Sherman's TG 38.3 encountered the most valuable target off Qui Nhon north of Cam Ranh. This was convoy HI-86 with nine merchants and a heavy escort. The convoy had departed Cape St Jacques on January 9 and was headed north. The escort comprised light cruiser *Kashii* and five *kaibokan*. Late on January 11, it reached Qui Nhon Bay and anchored. After leaving Qui Nhon Bay, it was discovered by TG 38.3. In two large attacks, aircraft from *Essex*, *Ticonderoga*, *Langley*, and *San Jacinto* laid waste to the convoy.

None of the nine merchant ships in the convoy survived this onslaught. Cargo ships *Yoshu Maru* and *Eiman Maru* (loaded with bauxite and raw rubber), along with tanker *San Luis Maru*, were sunk. The other six ships were damaged and forced to beach. *Otsusan Maru* (a cargo ship converted to tanker), passenger-cargo ship *Tatebe Maru*, cargo ship *Kyokuun Maru*, cargo ship *Yusei Maru*, ore carrier *Tatsubato Maru*, and cargo ship *Banshu Maru No. 63* all became constructive total losses.

The escort for this large convoy met a similar fate. Light cruiser *Kashii* was hit amidships by a torpedo in the early afternoon. This was followed by two bomb hits aft that detonated her depth-charge magazine. *Kashii* sank stern first with 621 members of her crew; only 19 survived. *CD-23* was attacked north of Qui Nhon and sunk with her entire crew of 155 officers and men.

TF 38's Rampage, January 6–20, 1945

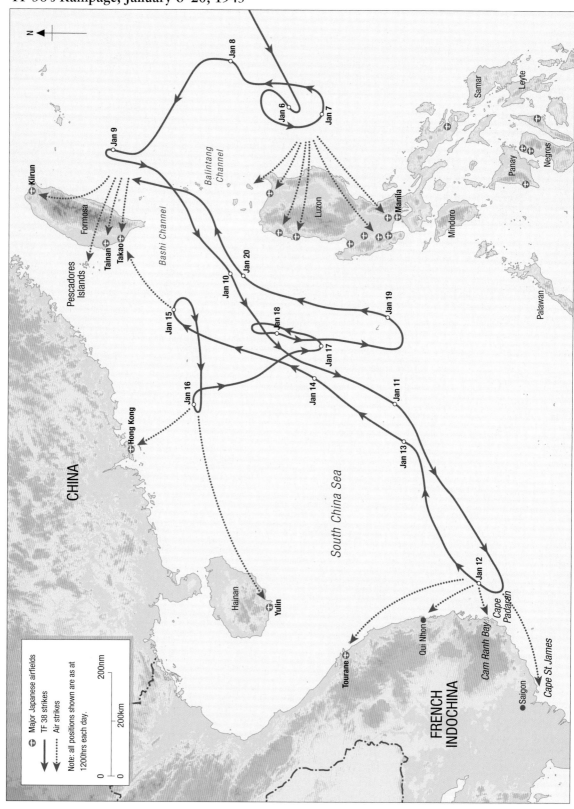

Legend:
- Major Japanese airfields
- TF 38 strikes
- Air strikes
- Note: all positions shown are as at 1200hrs each day.

0   200nm
0   200km

N

CHINA

Samar
Leyte
Negros
Panay
Mindoro
Palawan

Luzon
Manila

Balintang Channel

Bashi Channel

Kiirun
Formosa
Tainan
Takao
Pescadores Islands

Jan 6
Jan 7
Jan 8
Jan 9
Jan 10
Jan 11
Jan 12
Jan 13
Jan 14
Jan 15
Jan 16
Jan 17
Jan 18
Jan 19
Jan 20

Hong Kong

Hainan
Yulin

South China Sea

FRENCH INDOCHINA

Qui Nhon
Tourane
Cam Ranh Bay
Cape Padaran
Cape St James
Saigon

CD-51 suffered the same fate. After she blew up and sank, her depth charges detonated with fatal consequences for any survivors; 159 men were lost. From the entire convoy, only *kaibokan Daito* and *Ukuru*, and *CD-27* survived.

Aircraft from TG 38.2 found convoy SHISA-32 off Cape St James, which strikes from *Lexington*, *Hancock*, and *Hornet* proceeded to decimate. Tanker *Kumagawa Maru* was sunk (105 killed), as was tanker *Akashi Maru* (106 killed), which witnesses stated was hit by as many as ten torpedoes. Cargo ships *Kenei Maru* and *Kiyo Maru* were also assigned to the convoy; both were later sunk in Saigon. Three escorting *kaibokan* were sunk: *CD-17*, which was hit by three torpedoes and was lost with her entire crew of 159; *CD-19* (casualties unknown); and *Chiburi*, with 88 crewmen lost.

When convoy SATA-05 was located off Cape Paderan, another massacre ensued. SATA-05 consisted of tankers *Ayayuki Maru*, *Koshin Maru*, and *Eiho Maru* with cargo ships *Kensei Maru* and *Toyo Maru*. Landing ship *T.149* was detached from the convoy because of heavy seas, and survived. Escort for this important convoy with three tankers consisted of *CD-35*, *CD-43*, *Patrol Boat No. 103* (an ex-USN minesweeper), minesweeper *W-101*, and *Submarine Chaser Number 31*. The entire convoy was sunk. *CD-35* was hit by three bombs and sank with 69 men. *CD-43* was damaged by near misses that disabled her steering; she was beached on an uninhabited island and later blown up by her crew.

In addition to the destruction of these three convoys, other ships were found and attacked along bays and inlets on the coast of Indochina or in the large port of Saigon. Ships sunk in the vicinity of Cam Ranh Bay included *Submarine Chaser Number 43* and auxiliary minesweeper *Otowa Maru*.

Tanker *Shoei Maru*, and cargo ships *Tatsuhato Maru* and *Yujo Maru* were sunk north of Qui Nhon. Tankers *Ayanami Maru* and *Hoei Maru* went down southeast of Cape St James. The exact location of the sinking of tanker *Nanryu Maru No.2* went unrecorded. The following ships were sunk in the vicinity of Saigon: *T.140*, stores ship *Ikutagawa Maru*, transport *Kembu*

Maru, IJA cargo ships *France Maru* and *Shinsei Maru Number 17*, cargo ship *Taikyu Maru*, and tanker *Horai Maru Number 9*.

In addition to the massive damage to Japanese shipping, TF 38 claimed 113 Japanese aircraft destroyed in the air and on the ground. Total cost to the Americans was 23 aircraft lost.

At the conclusion of these strikes, Halsey claimed 41 ships sunk. This was remarkably close to the best available calculation of 11 IJN ships and 30 merchants lost. In any event, this was an unprecedented toll on shipping for a single day.

The following day, refueling was accomplished despite the rough weather. King gave directions from Washington that Halsey was to remain in a position to protect Lingayen Gulf from potential Japanese heavy forces approaching from the north or south. On January 14, with final refueling complete, TF 38 moved north to strike Formosa the following morning. Given the continuing heavy weather, McCain recommended that the strike be canceled. Halsey ordered that the strike go ahead.

From a position 170nm from Formosa, TF 38 launched a series of strikes at 0730hrs. A total of 16 fighter sweeps were directed at airfields on mainland China and Formosa. Despite this level of effort, only 16 Japanese aircraft were destroyed in the air and a paltry 18 on the ground. Strikes against shipping were more successful, but still had to contend with the low ceiling and heavy antiaircraft fire. The port of Takao in southern Formosa was observed to be full of shipping. The old Kamikaze-class destroyer *Hatakaze* was sunk, along with transport *T.14*. The old second-class destroyer *Tsuga* was spotted at Mako in the Pescadores and sunk.

On January 16, the focus turned to shipping at Hong Kong. Weather was a continuing problem, and Japanese antiaircraft fire demonstrated a growing effectiveness. A handful of merchants were sunk in Hong Kong harbor.

TF 38 paid a heavy price for this with 49 aircraft lost, 27 to operational causes and 22 from enemy action.

Halsey's original plan was to take TF 38 out of the South China Sea through the Luzon Strait. As the weather got worse over the course of January 17–18, Halsey revised this and planned an exit through Surigao Strait instead. When notified of this change, Nimitz recommended that TF 38 stick to its original plan to move through the Luzon Strait, but also made clear the final decision was up to Halsey. Taking TF 38 out of the war for a week with a long transit through the southern Philippines (where it would be exposed to air attack in restricted waters) was not sound planning, and Nimitz was also worried that the IJN might make a sudden move to interfere with the Lingayen Gulf landings. Throughout the campaign, he was concerned with a potential IJN move with its remaining capital ships, again demonstrating the utility of a "fleet in being" strategy. Halsey wisely deferred to his superior; he refueled on January 19 in calmer waters to the south and then headed north to transit the Luzon Strait on the 20th.

On January 21, TF 38 planned another series of strikes on Formosa, the Pescadores, and the southern Ryukyus. The much-improved weather allowed for a total of 1,164 offensive sorties. After the usual opening round of fighter sweeps, the morning focused on the destruction of shipping. Takao was still flush with targets; ten merchants were sunk. The afternoon strike focused on airfields and 104 Japanese aircraft were claimed to have been destroyed on the ground.

For the first time since November 1944, TF 38 felt the sting of kamikazes. Operating just 100nm east of Formosa, TF 38 was not difficult to find. Just after noon, a single aircraft appeared to conduct a conventional bombing attack on TG 38.3's light carrier *Langley*. One bomb hit forward. Personnel casualties were light, but the carrier was conducting flight operations three hours later. Within minutes, another aircraft also evaded radar detection and

This is probably one of the three tankers of SATA-05, left burning by *Lexington* aircraft on January 12. The heavy loss of tankers during Halsey's South China Sea raid dealt a significant blow to the Japanese war economy. (Naval Historical and Heritage Command)

At the end of Third Fleet's rampage into the South China Sea, the Special Attack Corps finally caught up with TF 38. On January 21, TG 38.3 came under attack from a mixed force of Zero and Judy kamikazes. *Ticonderoga* was hit twice by kamikazes and *Langley* was hit by a bomb. In this view, fire teams aboard *Langley* can be seen in action while *Ticonderoga* burns in the background. (Naval Historical and Heritage Command)

the CAP to commence a suicide dive against *Ticonderoga*. The kamikaze struck the flight deck and penetrated where its bomb exploded. An impending strike was spotted and ready to launch; now these aircraft provided fuel for the fire which was quickly spreading.

Just before 1300hrs, another group of eight kamikazes and five escorts resumed the attack on TG 38.3. Only two suicide aircraft survived the CAP to dive on the wounded *Ticonderoga*. One was sent spinning into the water by antiaircraft fire, but the final attacker crashed into the carrier's island. More fires were started. The crew succeeded in putting out the flames by 1415hrs and correcting a nine-degree list by 1800hrs. Though the ship was saved, the cost was high. Some 143 men were killed and 202, including her captain, were wounded. In addition, the air group lost 36 aircraft.

As a final farewell, kamikazes attacked the two destroyers on picket duty just 65nm off Formosa at 1310hrs. A single Zero had joined a returning strike. Before it could be identified as enemy, it dove on destroyer *Maddox*, striking her amidships. This and the explosion of the bomb aboard created a fire that was quickly extinguished.

After a final day of strikes on January 22 against the Ryukyus, TF 38 headed south to refuel, and then transited to the Ulithi, where it arrived on January 25. On January 26, Halsey turned over command of the Fast Carrier Force to Admiral Raymond Spruance. TF 38, now part of the Fifth Fleet and redesignated TF 58, had fought the Japanese and bad weather almost continuously since October 1944.

AFTERMATH AND ANALYSIS

The successful landing at Lingayen Gulf led to the liberation of Luzon. But more landings followed the Lingayen Gulf operation. On January 29, a corps was landed north of the Bataan peninsula to seal it off. Just two days later, a division was delivered south of Manila Bay to start a line of advance on the capital from a different direction. Prodded by MacArthur, American troops entered Manila on the evening of February 3. Despite Yamashita's orders to leave the city undefended, a garrison of up to 20,000 men, mostly naval troops, turned the city into a fortress. These die-hard defenders were not cleared until March 4, and only after the city was leveled and its citizens subjected to mass executions by the IJN troops.

Japanese naval troops were encountered again on Corregidor. The attack on the well-fortified island on February 16 encountered heavy resistance. Supported by 16 gunfire support ships, the combined paratroop and sea assault cleared the island by February 26. Legaspi in southern Luzon was attacked on April 1 in order to open San Bernardino Strait to shipping. The remaining Japanese on Luzon held out in the mountains on the northern part of the island until the end of the war. Yamashita and over 50,000 of his men surrendered on August 15.

MacArthur was not content with the liberation of Leyte, Mindoro, and Luzon. Though not officially sanctioned by the Joint Chiefs of Staff, MacArthur planned and executed the liberation of the central and southern Philippines. Kinkaid and Barbey ably supported these final mop-up operations. Japanese resistance was sporadic since they lacked air or naval forces to attack the invasion forces. When the Americans landed, the Japanese usually fell back to positions in the mountains to mount a prolonged defense. From February 28 until April 17, Barbey's forces conducted seven major amphibious operation and many more subsidiary ones.

ANALYSIS

The Japanese plan to conduct the decisive battle for the Philippines on and around Leyte was ill conceived and stood no chance of success. Once the IJN was defeated, as it was going to be given the balance of forces, the IJA had no means to sustain a fight on Leyte. The IJN's supreme effort to move troops to Leyte brought the Japanese garrison there to between 60,000 and 70,000 men. However, this force was up against an American force of more than 250,000 men at its peak. Though the battle for Leyte took

The introduction and extensive use of the kamikaze during the Philippines campaign changed the nature of the naval war for the last ten months of the Pacific conflict. In spite of the efforts of the Japanese to increase the tempo of kamikaze attacks, they were never able to change the course of the war. This is a Zero about to crash near *Essex* off Okinawa on May 14, 1945. (Naval Historical and Heritage Command)

much longer and required greater forces than MacArthur anticipated, the battle could only have one result. The process of being defeated on Leyte cost the IJN most of its remaining strength in the Philippines, and the IJA its best units located there. As a result, the defense of Luzon was crippled.

With few naval or air resources, the Japanese resorted to suicide attacks as their main weapon. Throughout the Philippines campaign, kamikazes exacted a heavy toll but could only generate tactical effects. For the expenditure of 500–600 aircraft, kamikazes damaged some 140 ships and craft, of which 17 were sunk or scuttled. The largest ship to be sunk was an escort carrier. Other ships sunk included three destroyers, a fast transport, six amphibious ships or craft, three other small combatants, and three merchant ships. Combined with the number of ships damaged, this was a significant toll. Even this scale of losses had no operational or strategic impact. As a military weapon, the kamikaze was ineffective in achieving its goal.

The primary kamikaze target was American aircraft carriers. These were potentially vulnerable targets since they carried ready sources of combustible items to start and sustain a conflagration, like fuel lines and aircraft loaded with fuel and ordnance. This danger was acute aboard escort carriers which lacked the fire-fighting capabilities and large damage-control crews of fleet carriers. Against TF 38 during the Philippines campaign, kamikazes hit Essex-class fleet carriers six times. None of these were in any danger of sinking. TF 38 was staggered during the campaign but was able to continue its critical mission of providing support to MacArthur's forces.

By 1944, the Japanese had no good options to mount a successful defense of the Philippines. Instead of committing everything to defend against the American landing at Leyte, they should have built up their forces for a defense of Luzon. Losing Leyte did not close the shipping lanes from Japan to its southern resource areas, but losing Luzon would. Had the IJN withheld its surface forces, strengthened its carrier force, and built up its land-based air power, a landing on Luzon would have been a much more costly affair for the Americans than it was. The cost of any invasion on Luzon would have been exponentially increased had the Japanese been able to mount a large-scale kamikaze campaign from the start. The IJA should have also built up its land-based air force and the means for its ground forces to prolong the fight. Had they prepared properly, the Japanese could have made the fight for Luzon even longer and more deadly than the battle for Okinawa.

The USN fought a victorious campaign to liberate the Philippines, but its performance was not without blemishes. It failed to secure the waters around Leyte in the aftermath of its crushing victory at the Battle of Leyte. The USN could not fathom that in the immediate aftermath of their crushing defeat, the Japanese were intent on reinforcing Leyte instead of withdrawing from it. MacArthur's intelligence staff was unclear as to Japanese intentions but assessed that a withdrawal was more likely. As a result, the Japanese were able to get the jump on the Americans and move significant reinforcements to the island and prolong the fight.

The Americans were also caught off guard by the appearance of the kamikaze. The old methods which had proved so successful in defeating conventional air attack were proven to be incapable of dealing with suicide attack. After a rough start, performance against kamikaze attack improved, but even as defenses against suicide attack were being refined, the cost was still high, as proved to be the case off Okinawa. The saving grace for the USN in this regard was the relatively small number of suicide aircraft available to the Japanese during the Philippines campaign.

The bright spots for the USN during the campaign were the ones that led to victory. The Philippines campaign provided a masterclass in amphibious warfare and how to manage the logistics required to keep a large fleet in the fight over a prolonged period. Despite Halsey's uneven handling of TF 38, it remained the most important and powerful piece on the naval chessboard and one to which the Japanese had no answer.

BIBLIOGRAPHY

Barbey, Daniel E., *MacArthur's Amphibious Navy: Seventh Amphibious Force Operations 1943–45*, Naval Institute Press, Annapolis, MD (1969)

Canon, M. Hamlin, *United States Army in World War II: The War in the Pacific, Leyte: The Return to the Philippines*, Office of the Chief of Military History, Department of the Army, Washington, DC (1954)

Craven, Wesley F. and James L. Cate (eds), *The Army Air Forces in World War II*, Vol. V: *The Pacific: Matterhorn to Nagasaki, June 1944 to August 1944*, Office of the Air Force History, Washington, DC (1983)

Dull, Paul S., *A Battle History of the Imperial Japanese Navy (1941–1945)*, Naval Institute Press, Annapolis, MD (1978)

GHQ, Southwest Pacific Area, *General Douglas MacArthur's Historical Report on Allied Operations in the Southwest Pacific Area*, Vols. I–II, Government Printing Office, Washington, DC (1966)

Inoguchi, Rikihei and Tadashi Nakajima, with Roger Pineau, *The Divine Wind: Japan's Kamikaze Force in World War II*, Naval Institute Press, Annapolis, MD (1994)

Japanese Monograph No. 12, *4th Air Army Operations, 1944–1945*

Japanese Monograph No. 81, *Philippines Area Naval Operations, Part III, Dec. 1944–Jan. 1945*

Japanese Monograph No. 84, *Philippines Area Naval Operations, Part II, Oct.–Dec. 1944*

Japanese Monograph No. 114, *Philippines Area Naval Operations, Part IV, Jan.–Aug. 1945*

Morison, Samuel Eliot, *History of United States Naval Operations in World War II*, Vol. XII: *Leyte June 1944–January 1945*, Little, Brown and Company, Boston, MA (1974)

Morison, Samuel Eliot, *History of United States Naval Operations in World War II*, Vol. XIII: *The Liberation of the Philippines, Luzon, Mindanao, the Visayas 1944–1945*, Little, Brown and Company, Boston, MA (1975)

O'Hara, Vincent P., *The U.S. Navy Against the Axis*, Naval Institute Press, Annapolis, MD (2007)

Reynolds, Clark, *The Fast Carriers*, Naval Institute Press, Annapolis, MD (1992)

Rielly, Robin L., *Kamikaze Attacks of World War II*, McFarland & Company, Inc., Publishers, Jefferson, NC (2010)

Smith, Robert R., *United States Army in World War II: The War in the Pacific, Triumph in the Philippines*, Office of the Chief of Military History, Department of the Army, Washington, DC (1984)

Stern, Robert C., *Fire from the Sky*, Naval Institute Press, Annapolis, MD (2010)

Wheeler, Gerald R., *Kinkaid of the Seventh Fleet*, Naval Institute Press, Annapolis, MD (1996)

Yeo, Mike, *Desperate Sunset*, Osprey Publishing Ltd, Oxford (2019)

Websites:

www.combinedfleet.com

INDEX

Figures in **bold** refer to maps and images.